Multicultural Kingdom

Multicultural Kingdom

Ethnic Diversity, Mission and the Church

Harvey Kwiyani

scm press

© Harvey Kwiyani 2020

Published in 2020 by SCM Press
Editorial office
3rd Floor, Invicta House,
108–114 Golden Lane,
London EC1Y 0TG, UK
www.scmpress.co.uk

SCM Press is an imprint of Hymns Ancient & Modern Ltd
(a registered charity)

Hymns Ancient & Modern® is a registered trademark of
Hymns Ancient & Modern Ltd
13A Hellesdon Park Road, Norwich,
Norfolk NR6 5DR, UK

978-0-334-05752-9

British Library Cataloguing in Publication data

A catalogue record for this book is available
from the British Library

Scripture quotations from New Revised Standard Version Bible: Anglicized
Edition, copyright © 1989, 1995 National Council of the Churches of Christ in
the United States of America. Used by permission. All rights reserved worldwide.

Bible extracts taken from the New King James Version® are copyright © 1982 by
Thomas Nelson. Used by permission. All rights reserved.

Contents

To Eric Msampha
and to Gabriel Diya

my brothers
my friends
gone too soon.
You are greatly missed.

Acknowledgements

This book summarizes a conversation that has been on my mind for a very long time. The subject of cultural diversity in the worldwide Christian community has been of great interest to me for the past 20 years. In this time, I have had the privilege to live and work with Christians in quite a few Western cities, from Saint Gallen in Switzerland to Saint Paul in Minnesota, and from Nottingham to Oxford to Liverpool, here in the United Kingdom. Thus, my thoughts on the subject being discussed in this book have been shaped by countless opportunities I have had to interact with Christians from Europe and North America, to observe and ask questions especially about Christian mission in the context of segregated Christianity in the West.

I have drawn insight from numerous people – too many to count. However, I have to mention a few friends. I am deeply grateful to Alexander and Annette Teifenthaler of Feldkirch in Austria for both opening the door to Europe for me and for acting on their faith that God uses people of all races. Without their trust and help, my journey would have been very different. I am also thankful to Christopher Daza for helping me make sense of the segregated Christianity that I first saw in Europe in 2000. He helped me develop the initial argument for the anti-segregation missiology that appears in this book. Here in England, I am greatly indebted to Philip Mountstephen, Paul Thaxter, Jonny Baker and Cathy Ross, and Colin Smith who made a home for me at the Church Mission Society (CMS) in Oxford and modelled for me the intentionality required to diversify mission teams to reflect the global nature of God's kingdom. During my stay in Minnesota, USA, I was nourished by the works of such scholars as John Perkins and Virgilio Elizondo, both of whom are pioneers in this discourse. Their dream of a desegregated Church is what informs my vision for a multicultural kingdom. Their words helped me continue on my path when I experienced racial marginalization especially among my white Evangelical friends in the United States.

I also have to thank my many students of mission who are scattered across the country – maybe the world. I am certain I learned more from them than they did from me. Their questions on the subject of 'race and the mission of God' allowed me space to critically reflect on some of the issues discussed in this book. Without them, this book would not be what it is.

Finally, I have to thank my parents, the Reverends Jonathan and Hilda Kwiyani of Chiradzulu in Malawi. Their ministerial experience and wisdom often prove helpful to my process of writing. I am blessed to have them around. Also, my three *schatzilles*, Nancy, Rochelle and Roxanne. Their hope for a more desegregated kingdom will one day be answered.

While writing this book, I lost two very close friends, Eric Msampha and Gabriel Diya. It is to their memory that I dedicate the book. Their passion for the work of the ministry will live on.

mosaic /mə(ʊ)'zeɪɪk/

noun: mosaic; plural noun: mosaics

- a picture or pattern produced by arranging together small pieces of stone, tile, glass, etc. For example: 'mosaics on the interior depict scenes from the Old Testament'.

I

The Kingdom of God is Like a Mosaic

After this I looked, and there was a great multitude that no one could count, from every nation, from all tribes and peoples and languages, standing before the throne and before the Lamb, robed in white, with palm branches in their hands. (Rev. 7.9)

I usually discuss my missiological writings with my mother. Her name is Hilda, and she lives in Malawi where she has led a congregation for more than 30 years together with my father, Jonathan. I find her to be a great critical sounding board who helps me disentangle some of my thoughts when they become convoluted. Her experience and wisdom have been significantly helpful to me along my journey of thinking about mission in a context that is extremely different from where I grew up. The first time I brought to her the argument of this book, she was both excited and perplexed. She was excited because she hoped to get some theological insights out of this book to help her shape the multicultural community that she leads in rural Chiradzulu, in southern Malawi. Diversity for her and her community is a social phenomenon that happens naturally without any theological intentionality, and she hoped that in this endeavour she could find ways to embed her praxis in solid theological foundations.

Yet she was also perplexed, because to her cultural diversity among Christians is a given. There is no other way to conceive of the *ekklesia* apart from it being a multicultural community of followers of Christ worshipping and serving God wherever they have been scattered around the world. After a few days of careful reflection on the subject of this book, she asked me: 'What do you mean when you say a multicultural kingdom?' She needed an explanation because as far as she is concerned it does not make sense for one kingdom to have two cultures. The kingdoms that she knows, especially those in southern Africa, have one culture, or something extremely close to one culture. They are established around a set of kingdom-wide values and languages that make it impossible for people to have more than one culture. No sane king would allow a multiplicity of cultures in his kingdom. A few days after this conversation, my mother called me to correct herself. She had realized that cultural diversity among Christians in the world means exactly this – the kingdom of God is elastic enough to hold all cultures of the world. Indeed, the kingdom of God is one in which all nations, tribes and tongues belong. She gave me an example that drove the point home; the United Kingdom is one such kingdom. The English, Scottish, Welsh and Northern Irish live together under one monarchy.

Still, she was bewildered to hear that Christianity here in Europe and North America has not yet figured out how the nations, tribes and tongues can belong together in worship, that the body of Christ in the West is segregated, that even among African Christians in Europe and North America it is almost impossible to have a multicultural church. She could not understand that in the West, generally speaking, black Christians worship with fellow black Christians; white Christians worship with fellow white Christians; the same goes for Latin American and Asian Christians. She was taken aback when I told her of the 'black majority churches' in London (which is a more generous way of describing Nigerian congregations, Ghanaian congregations, Congolese congregations, and many others). 'Why do you have to qualify the nature of a congregation by race, ethnicity or nationality? How can that be?' she wondered. I told her that both in the United Kingdom and in the United States, more than 85 per cent of *all* congregations are made up of people of the same race (and usually of the same social status). Suddenly, she remembered some words of Martin Luther King: 'Sunday morning is the most segregated hour of the week.' I said that Sunday morning is still the most segregated hour today, just as it was 50 years ago. She went quiet on the phone for a few moments, and then, in a disappointed motherly tone, she said, 'Tell your friends, you do not know what you are missing.'

My mother lives in rural Malawi and so her concern for cultural diversity is not based on racial segregation – she probably has never had a racist encounter in her adult life (she spent her first 15 years on a colonial farm in Zimbabwe). Her immediate context understands cultural diversity in ethnic and tribal terms. (And yes, I use the word 'tribe'. It is high time we redeemed it from its pejorative colonial baggage. My evangelical friends will be glad to hear that it is also biblical.)[1] Indeed, cultural diversity for most of the world is a tribal or an ethnic phenomenon. I still remember the child in Austria who almost fainted when he saw me because he had never seen a black person before. He could not resist the urge to touch me to see if I was real, and then in utter amazement looked at his hand to see if it was black from my skin. An overwhelming majority of the world's population never have to deal with significant cross-racial relations. Yet, my mother's concern is not even about tribal segregation. People in my home area do not segregate or discriminate –

as far as I know – on tribal or ethnic grounds. Many of them have been neighbours for ages even though they belong to different ethnicities and, sometimes, religions. They have shared their lives together for generations – many have intermarried across tribal lines and cannot certainly say what their tribal identity is. They may speak several languages, some of which are not their own tribal languages, and they do this just to be able to communicate with their neighbours. My family is a good example. My mother is a Yao by tribe, and is married to a Lhomwe, but neither she nor my father speak their tribal languages well. My siblings and I were raised speaking chiChewa, a tribal language of the Chewa peoples. My mother is aware that in other parts of Malawi, and in other countries in southern Africa, inter-tribal relations are not this cordial. She has therefore often wondered about the power of the gospel to help tribal and ethnic rivals to reconcile. One day she asked me if I thought we needed to look to theology to find help to stop inter-tribal violence.

In my parents' church and in the wider region of southern Malawi, Christians from the various tribes worship together several times a week. Worship in the congregations where my parents live happens in a mixture of languages. It is common for people to sing Lhomwe and Yao songs in worship, say their intercession in chiSena or chiTumbuka, and then listen to a sermon in chiChewa. When they sing Yao songs, the accompanying musical instruments and their body movements will mimic Yao music and dance – *manganje* worship is the best. This is normal – Lhomwe, Sena, Tonga, Nkhonde worship will also be shaped by their cultures. On any Sunday, in one service, people will experience some combination of these cultural expressions of Christianity. My mother reflected on this beautiful reality for a while. It was one of those things that is there in front of your eyes, but you don't see it until you are looking. Suddenly, it hit her. She exclaimed, 'That is the point of the Church, and of Christianity. I can assure you, there is no other platform in our area where people get to enjoy the best of other cultures as we do in our worship. This only happens in church.' When I pressed her to explain how it all works, she said, 'It is like a jigsaw puzzle. You only see the full image once all the pieces are in place.' My six-year-old daughter then joined in the conversation: 'I think you mean a mosaic, Grandma.' My mother replied, 'The kingdom of God is like a mosaic. The beauty comes out of each piece being in its right place and contributing its colours – and all the pieces, in their magnificent colours, are needed for the mosaic to be a mosaic.' This was her concern – the full beauty of the kingdom of God can only be seen when the pieces line up. I realized that this is a very important conversation for Christians in the West to take on board. Our segregated Christianity is an anomaly and it is my sincere hope that we will not export it to the rest of the world like we have other aspects of our Christianity in the past.

The Church is God's global mosaic

The Oxford dictionary defines 'mosaic' as 'a picture or pattern produced by arranging together small pieces of stone, tile, glass, etc.' A mosaic is usually a decorative piece of art made by arranging together differently coloured, shaped or sized stones, tiles or other materials in a pattern to portray an image. Mosaics have been around for many centuries. They were commonly used in both the Greek and the Roman empires. They were also present in early Christian basilicas. They can still be seen on domes, walls and floors of cathedrals around Europe. They also decorate other religious buildings, including in Islam, and important political buildings, such as castles and palaces. Ancient mosaics were made of stone or ceramic tesserae; modern ones often use synthetic materials, even plastic tiles.

I find the metaphor of the mosaic helpful on many levels. First, for there to be a mosaic there must be an artist who has an idea of what the mosaic should look like when complete. The artist must have the finished design in mind and a plan on how to build it. The mosaic must look a certain way and therefore specific tiles have to be used and positioned in their rightful places. The artist then has to find the right sizes and colours of those specific tiles, pebbles, stones, and any other materials necessary to make their mosaic. There is also a need for glue, cement or other substance to hold the pieces in place. The artist needs to know where to fit each piece to bring out the best from it, to complement the pieces close to it and enhance the overall beauty of the entire mosaic. The ultimate goal is to create a piece of art that is pleasing to the eye. The pieces, whatever their colour or size, serve one purpose – to produce an image according to the artist's plan.

In the argument of this book, the mosaic is the kingdom of God, the body of Christ, the fellowship of the Spirit, scattered to all parts of the world. The Spirit is the glue keeping us together by holding us close to each other and at the same time giving us gifts for one another. God is the artist making the mosaic. God is its owner too. Only God can own and make the mosaic – only God has the entire picture of what the mosaic should look like in the end, with the image of God's Son revealed through it. We are all tiles in God's hand. God is the one putting us together. God decides and determines where best to fit each tile, for God alone has the plan of what the mosaic will look like when finished. One tile cannot make a mosaic. Nor can tiles of just one type. Other constrasting pieces are needed to create something beautiful. Essentially, God is building a kingdom in which people of many national, tribal or linguistic identities belong together. It is not a monocultural kingdom: all cultures are invited and all cultures are needed. It is not a monoracial kingdom: all races are welcome. It is not a colour-blind kingdom. It does not see one human race but sees us all as who we really are: Africans, Asians, Europeans, everybody. It expects us all to bring our unique gifts to make the kingdom what it is meant to be – the kingdom of Jesus, the Lord of the nations.

A kingdom of many cultures

My mother's reaction made me realize that the argument at the centre of this book, that the kingdom of God is a kingdom of many cultures, is both extremely easy to grasp and counter-intuitive at the same time. On the one hand, it makes perfect sense. This kingdom of God – the kingdom of *our* God – cannot be monocultural because God created this diverse universe in which we live. Every time God creates something new and different, it is to be declared good. We see this in the book of Genesis. It is very likely that God loves diversity. There are 7 billion of us in the world today and no two people are exactly the same. Even the universe testifies: there are millions upon millions of species that God has designed to exist together in harmony. Yet God invites people from all nations, tribes and tongues into God's kingdom and does not demand that they abandon who they are in order to belong to the kingdom. They ought to be able to come into the kingdom bringing with them the flavours from their cultures to embellish this great fellowship of the Spirit that is the kingdom of God. Indeed, the kingdom is big enough to accommodate all peoples of the earth. It is elastic enough to allow for people of all nationalities, tribes and languages to enter in to worship God. Essentially, God anticipates that all cultures will find their way into the kingdom, and on the rare occasions when people from a culture not yet represented enter, the kingdom simply expands to make space for them, showing them and learning from them how to follow Christ. It is quite difficult to argue for a monocultural expression of the kingdom of God.

On the other hand, a kingdom of many cultures should not make sense. How can a kingdom have many cultures? Allowing more than one culture to exist in a kingdom is disaster. Earthly kingdoms generally have one shared culture with a common language and worldview. Not many kingdoms survive with several cultures. As long as there is one king or queen, the kingdom is likely to be shaped by one culture. Whatever the governing monarch decides is what goes throughout the kingdom. If there are any minority cultures within the kingdom, they are subsumed and therefore changed by the dominant culture of the kingdom. There is no room for divergence. You either belong or you are out. You either fit in or you will be rejected.

Christianity, by its very nature, must be multicultural. It must wrestle with the universal invitation that Christ gives to the nations to come into his kingdom. Central to Christianity's missionary calling is the belief that it is God's desire that all may be saved. In his first letter to Timothy, Paul advises that supplication, prayers and intercession have to be made for rulers to allow for peace in the land, and then adds, 'For this is right and acceptable in the sight of God our Saviour, who desires everyone to be saved and to come to the knowledge of the truth' (1 Tim. 2.3–4). We also remember Jesus' words, 'to go to all the nations and make disciples'. That 'all' includes people from every cultural group and nationality in the world, from Aborigines to Bavarians to Chileans all the way to Zulus, and everyone else in between. Indeed, God is no respecter of persons, Jesus Christ is Lord of all, and the Spirit of God has been poured upon all flesh. As Christians from various tribes and tongues, we have one Lord, one faith and one baptism. We have all been adopted into *one* kingdom of God, and there is only one kingdom of God.

Organization of the book

The argument of this book is explored in three stages. The next two chapters explore the historical development of the circumstances around the coming of the new missional era of cultural diversity in Britain. Making use of the larger story of the spread of Christianity through the missionary movement, first from Europe and North America to the rest of the world (1792 to about 1970), and then from anywhere in the world to practically anywhere else (1970 onwards), I attempt to paint a picture of how a new Christian cultural diversity has come about in Britain. British Christians and missionaries went to the rest of the world, and now many Christians from the rest of the world have made Britain their home. I use the two World Missionary Conferences of 1910 and 2010 as bookends to the story that started out with little or no diversity yet 100 years later cannot rightly be told without acknowledging diversity. The middle chapters begin to explore the implications of this diversity in our understanding of the Church, the world and the other. If Christ is Lord of all, how do we as Christ's followers engage one another in our different tribal and cultural groupings? Exploring the theme of migration, I discuss what happens when Christian tribes from around the world find themselves in the same city, serving the same people. Towards the end of the book, I make an argument that where there is cultural diversity in general society, Christian churches must make the effort to reflect the diversity in their membership. Believing that cultural diversity is a gift from God, and that God calls us to be hospitable to others, I conclude that multicultural congregations are the way forward in the West.

It is the folly of our time that we have reasons to justify segregating churches.

Note

1 I would be happy to use the word 'nation' (Gk *ethne*) instead of 'tribe' (Gk *fylí*), but for the sake of this discourse, where I use 'nation' I refer to a collection of tribes. For instance, the nation of Israel includes 12 tribes.

2

The Great New Fact of Our Era

I have a friend in London called Bankole. He is a medical doctor and works for the NHS. He is also a leader in a Church of England congregation in south-east London. He is of Nigerian origin, of Yoruba heritage, which he takes rather too seriously. He refuses to use his English name (which, incidentally, is his Christian name) even though it appears on both his birth certificate and his passport. His dress is typically Nigerian: he has more *agbadas* than he has suits. They give him his identity. Without them, he is not himself. His wife is known for her exquisite collection of Nigerian headgear – she has one to suit every occasion. All his children are called by their Nigerian names only, and he insists that they are pronounced correctly, with the accents in the right places. In his house, only Yoruba is allowed. Thus, he has successfully taught his children Yoruba even though they were all born and raised in London. Yet, he identifies as a Christian first, before Yoruba. In his heart, his Christian identity is more important. Above everything, he yearns to be recognized as a Christian Yoruba man. His entire family takes great pride in these two aspects of their life: their Christian faith and their Nigerian/Yoruba identity. Since first coming to London he has stubbornly attempted to embody, at all times, what it means to be a Christian and a Nigerian at the same time in a multicultural city.

Bankole was born into a Christian family at a Christian hospital near Lagos in the 1950s. St Luke's Hospital was – and still is – a mission hospital established by the Church Missionary Society (CMS), a British mission society that had a great presence in West Africa a hundred years ago. Bankole's English name was given in honour of one of the lead CMS missionaries at the hospital who remains a legendary figure both in Nigeria and in Britain today. Bankole's parents and his grandparents worked at St Luke's. His grandparents worked for many years as grounds staff, while his father was a hospital administrator and his mother was a nurse at St Luke's all their working lives. Bankole grew up in the hospital grounds, playing with the children of British missionaries who ran the hospital. He was lucky enough to go to the only international school in the area, which was mainly for the children of colonial expatriates and missionaries. He grew up hearing missionary stories, especially in the time leading up to Nigeria's independence – which would be followed by a civil war, a situation that forced many missionaries to leave Nigeria. He became aware, even as a young boy, of the changing fortunes of Christian mission agencies – the effects on mission and the missionaries when the colonized states became independent. He had heard about the declining numbers of Christians in Europe before he came to England to study medicine. He understood while he was still in Nigeria that most Western mission agencies were finding it hard to recruit new missionaries or to raise financial support for missionaries already working around the world. However, after several years of living in Britain, as a medical student and then as a doctor, he came to believe that Britain needs him here as a missionary more than Nigeria needs him as a doctor.

London needs spiritual doctors

Bankole intended to return to Nigeria upon the completion of his studies to lead St Luke's Hospital. When I met him in London, the plans of going back had been on hold for more than 20 years. When he is asked why he has not returned to Nigeria, he always says that London needs more doctors for the souls of men and women – missionaries – to heal them of secularism, consumerism, individualism, and many other 'isms' (like racism) and therefore he is needed in London much more than at St Luke's. The irony is striking. Bankole has come from St Luke's to become a missionary and a doctor in London. He says jokingly that a hundred years ago the heathens were in Nigeria (among other parts of the world) and Britain rightly sent missionaries to evangelize them. Now, in the twenty-first century, the heathens are in Britain, and he is here to convert the British back to Christianity. It is very likely that the British missionaries who worked at St Luke's when Bankole was growing up would never have thought that Nigerians, let alone Bankole, would become missionaries in Britain. He says he will return to Nigeria soon, but not to lead St Luke's. Even though he is thoroughly Nigerian in his outlook, he has devoted his life (and that of his family) to the people of Britain. He not only wants them to hear the gospel, he also wants them to see that it is possible for a person to be an African and a Christian at the same time – that the British expression of Christianity is not the only one. Eventually, Bankole hopes to return to Nigeria when he retires. He wants to be laid to rest with his parents.

Bankole is right. Like the European missionaries who worked in Africa and other parts of the world in past centuries, people from the rest of the world now dedicate their lives to serving in mission in Britain. In the nineteenth and twentieth centuries, the mission field was understood to be Latin America, Africa and Asia, and the rest of the non-Western world. Of course, one can argue that Europe and North America were also mission fields, but in the Christendom understanding of mission at the time, the heathens were everywhere else apart from Europe and North America. Consequently, missionaries went from Europe and North America to evangelize in Latin America, Africa and Asia. Today, in the twenty-first century, the world looks different. Contemporary mission fields include Britain, Europe and, indeed, most of the Western world. Most Westerners are yet to realize this, but the heathen who need to be evangelized are in Europe today just as much as in anywhere else in the world. Bankole's mission field is London, where he serves people of many nationalities as both a medical doctor and a lay minister, but he is only one of many Christians from Africa, Asia and Latin America who have settled in Britain and are living out their faith serving British people.

Indeed, Bankole's story is not that unique. In the past 20 years, I have come across thousands of African, Asian and Latin American Christians in Britain, Germany, France, the United States, Canada, and practically all of the West, including Australia and New Zealand. My research on the missionary works of African Christians in the West led me to discover numerous African congregations scattered across Europe and North America. Other scholars such as Jehu Hanciles[1] and Afe Adogame[2] have come to similar conclusions: the presence of African Christians in the West has a significant impact on the religious landscape of many Western countries. I conducted my research more than ten years ago; since then both the presence and the social impact of African Christians in Europe have become more pronounced.

I have another friend called Kweku. He comes from Ghana and leads a church in Glasgow, a vibrant African congregation. He also works as an accountant in one of the major corporations in the city. He tells me that churches like his are where growth is happening, and that they are slowly becoming the most visible expressions of the Christian faith in Scotland. Sheila Akomiah-Conteh, a Ghanaian researcher in Scotland, agrees with Kweku. Her research of 2018, exploring church planting and church growth in Glasgow, found that over 75 per cent of new churches started in the city between 2000 and 2015 are African.[3] She concludes that the future of congregations in Glasgow looks African. Kweku is more pointed in his assessment: 'We keep Christianity going in Glasgow. Without us, Christianity has only a few generations before it disappears.' He may be overstating the case, but there is a general consensus that

British Christianity is becoming more diverse, with the African expression slowly rising in prominence.

That said, the presence of foreign Christians in Britain is not limited to Africans. The numbers of Latin American Christians and missionaries in British cities have also grown quite significantly in the past three decades. Filipe is a Brazilian who pastors a Portuguese-speaking church in Birmingham. He started his congregation in response to requests from the many Portuguese-speaking Christians in the city who needed a pastor who could minister to them in their language. His congregation is currently made up of Christians from Brazil, Portugal, Mozambique and Angola. The only uniting factor for Filipe's congregation is the language, even though sometimes they need interpretation from one Portuguese dialect to another – Brazilian Portuguese does not sound exactly like Angolan Portuguese. Having led the congregation for several years, he hopes to attract English speakers to his newly established English service, which is intended for the young people of his church who are not fluent in Portuguese. He has realized that his own teenage children are not keen to stay in the Portuguese church; they need an English service.

I should also mention my South Korean friend, Paul. His real name is Moong Bon, but he has learned to use what he calls his 'English name', which is easier for his British friends to pronounce. He has only reluctantly agreed to become Paul because of his zeal to preach the gospel in Europe. His church in Manchester currently caters to the Koreans in the Greater Manchester area, but he is keen to reach out to his neighbours irrespective of nationality. He believes that, much like Paul of the New Testament, he has been sent to the nations and he wants to be all things to all people. He thinks of himself as an apostle to the nations, but being in Manchester he has come to the conclusion that he can actually reach the world within Manchester itself. His assistant pastor, Wang Yong, is a Mandarin-speaking Chinese. Unlike Moong Bon, Wang Yong refuses to have an English name. He was quick to let me know: 'If you can pronounce Russian names, you can learn to pronounce Chinese names.' Together, Moong Bon and Wang Yong hope to have the largest Asian network of churches in Europe.

Diversity is the new normal

Thousands of foreign Christians have come to Britain over the past 50 years. Some migrated to Britain as international students, planning to return to their home countries after completing their studies, but instead stayed on after graduation, found employment and settled here. Many migrated as refugees because of adverse political and economic situations in their home countries, hoping to find safety here to raise their children and give them a better education. Still others came to Britain as highly skilled migrants for work and business opportunities. Whatever their reason for coming, they are here in Britain now, and they are contributing to the current religious landscape of the country. Their presence, in the ecclesial circles in Britain as they attend worship services each Sunday, in their workplaces within the week, or in their service as community organizers or on school boards, is slowly redefining what it means to be a Christian in Britain today. Unlike Bankole, many of them do not call themselves missionaries (in the professional sense of the word). They are simply Christian migrants who have found their way to Britain, and have brought their Christianity with them. The impact of their presence is seen all around. Christianity in Britain in the twenty-first century is a phenomenon of many cultures and races. When we talk about a British Christian today, we do not necessarily mean a *white* British Christian. Of course, a British Christian today may actually be of Nigerian, Korean, Filipino or Brazilian descent, and indeed of any skin colour. What we have called black, Asian and ethnic minority (BAME) Christians are slowly becoming a big minority.

This cultural diversity in British Christianity is the great new fact of our era. In addition to historically British denominations like the Church of England, Church of Scotland and the Methodist Church, British Christianity today includes within it – to mention just a few – the Redeemed Christian Church of God (from Nigeria), the Church of Pentecost (from Ghana), the Universal Church of the Kingdom of God (from Brazil), Roman Catholic Christians from Poland, and many Korean and Chinese fellowships scattered across the country. I was struck when, during ethnographic research in 2015 on the religious lives of younger Africans in Britain, a group of white British teenagers in Manchester explained to me that, as far as they could tell, it was not possible for white people to be Christians. Many of them were detached by two or three generations from Christianity and therefore had no close Christian friends. All the Christians they knew in their schools were people of other races. When I asked them what comes to mind when they hear the word 'Christian', they did not hesitate to mention the many BAME Christians and the migrant churches they see in their neighbourhoods. They associate the word 'Christian' with the Bible-carrying, tongue-speaking Nigerian Pentecostals who rent their school halls for church services, or the Polish Catholics who have made the Mass viable again in their neighbourhood parish. They could not believe that their ancestors took Christianity to Africa only 150 years ago.

Cultural diversity within the landscape of British Christianity is the new normal and is here to stay. There exists in every city across the country more than a few congregations of African, Asian, Latin American and many other foreign Christians. London, for instance, is home to Asian (Indian, South Korean, Filipino) and Latin American (Brazilian, Peruvian) Christians, in addition to the many African and Afro-Caribbean congregations scattered across the city in what have come to be called black majority churches. African Christianity is highly visible in London, it could be the most visible Christianity in the city. There is the famous Old Kent Road where there is a high concentration of African churches and ministries. However, Old Kent Road is not the only place where African churches are located. The entire region of south-east London is home to the highest concentration of African churches outside Africa. Out of this region has emerged a new African missionary movement that is sending missionaries to Africa and other parts of the world from Britain. The missionaries of the past centuries would not have foreseen this – that Africans would become the European missionaries evangelizing not only Africa but the world, from Europe.

We must also talk about the Redeemed Christian Church of God, which came to Britain from Nigeria where it was formed in 1952. Their first congregation in Britain was officially inaugurated in 1989. They currently have around 1,000 congregations across the United Kingdom. When they have their Festival of Life overnight prayer services (twice every year, first around Easter and then in October), they bring together over 50,000 Christians from the south-east of England to the London Excel, and it is streamed to millions of people around the world. Attending it, you might feel like you were at a big football match. It is put together by African Christians, generally speaking, for other Africans in London. They have other smaller – though still attracting 20,000 – Festival of Life gatherings in Manchester and in Cardiff where many other members of the RCCG get together for their own prayer vigils. The impact of the Festival of Life has become increasingly noticeable in the past decade; key British politicians sometimes attend to make use of the ready-made audience. David Cameron, for instance, attended the Festival of Life in London Excel in 2015 where he was given a chance to speak to the many thousands of people in attendance.

There is little doubt now that African Christianity is slowly becoming an important part of British Christianity. Peter Brierley writes that the London Church Census (2011) figures suggested that 49 per cent of people who went to church on any given Sunday in London were black African and Caribbean Christians.[4] Anecdotal reports put that figure at more than 60 per cent in 2019. Thus, in London today, people of African descent – who form only 14 per cent of the city's population – make up over 60 per cent of church attendance in the city.

This is not a statistic to be taken lightly especially as it is said, 'as London goes, so goes the nation'. This fact that the majority of church attendance in London is black while black people are a very small minority of London's population should cause us to reflect on several issues. Generally speaking, London Christianity is becoming black, or in other words, Christianity is becoming a black religion in London. This reshaping of Christianities in London will undoubtedly have a great impact on the entire British religious landscape. While many of the African and Afro-Caribbean Christians are in the Church of England, or in other British or 'white-majority' denominations (for instance, Baptists, Methodists, Vineyard), many more are in Pentecostal and Charismatic churches. Further, and I find this to be of great significance, the growth of African churches has almost single-handedly reversed the many years of church decline in London. In the years following 2008, research (largely from Peter Brierley) has suggested that London churches are growing again. Brierley's 2013 report entitled *London Churches Are Growing!* showed that there is a net increase in church attendance in London.[5] This followed Brierley's previous book, *Pulling Out of the Nosedive*, which picked up the trends much earlier.[6] A careful beneath-the-surface reading of both publications reveals that it is largely African and Afro-Caribbean churches that are growing in London – and they are growing fast enough to offset the overall decline that has been going on in the city for decades. Of course, it is not just in London where black churches are growing. In the midst of general membership decline across the country, black Evangelical, Charismatic and Pentecostal churches seem to be bucking the trend.

In a nutshell, Christian diversity in Britain is here to stay and it will most likely change both the British religious landscape and British Christianity for good. It will define a new missional era in Britain where many expressions of Christianity are coming into close contact with each other and are thus finding themselves having to figure out how to belong together across racial and cultural barriers and to collaborate in their efforts to continue evangelizing in Britain. Western theologians and church leaders often cite the decline of Christianity and the rise of post-modernity as the two major forces that have shaped the current Western missional context. While these are valid issues of concern, I propose that it is rather cultural diversity, resulting from the shrinking global village and the migration of millions of non-Western Christians to the West, that will have an even greater impact on the Western religious and cultural landscape in the twenty-first century. A well-informed forward-looking missional outlook suggests that cultural diversity will be a more prevalent force in the shaping of British Christianity in the future than anything else. We should not talk about mission in the West without considering cultural diversity – both Christians currently living in Britain, whatever organizations or denominations they belong to, and the general populace that we want to evangelize. Our discourse, be it the missional church conversation, the emerging church, missionary congregations, or fresh expressions of church, must reflect cultural diversity.

The emergence of a multicultural Christian community in Britain

Back in 1944, the Archbishop of Canterbury William Temple wrote in *The Church Looks Forward* that 'the coming of a Christian fellowship that extends into almost every nation in the world is the new great fact of our era'.[7] He had in mind the spreading of an overarching Western Christianity (dressed in the garb of European Christendom) out into the rest of the geopolitical world of the 1940s. Even Kenneth Latourette opened his *The Emergence of a World Christian Community* (published in 1949) with the observation that, 'One of the most striking facts of our time is the global extension of Christianity.'[8] Both these statements are true. The emergence of a world Christian community is indeed a significant milestone in the history of religion, and it ought to be recognized as such. It comes after a massive missionary effort by European and North American Christians who left the comfort and convenience of a Western life to evangelize the overwhelmingly unevangelized majority world of the time – and this too has to be appreciated. However, both the above statements were published at a time when on the one hand the Western missionary movement continued to attempt to replicate Western-styled Christianity and churches around the world, and on the other colonialism was still the order of the day for most of the rest of the world. In addition, in the eyes of those in the majority world there seemed to be little distinction between Western missionaries, traders and colonial agents. Because of this, Western Christianity was the template upon which world Christianity would be moulded. Consequently, the world Christianity celebrated by both William Temple and Kenneth Latourette in the 1940s, which in the words of Temple 'binds the citizens of the nations in true unity and mutual love',[9] ought to have looked exactly like Western Christianity but should have stayed in the colonies and the majority world. Traffic between the colonizing governments and the colonies always flowed in one direction. Little did they know that within the next 50 years everything would be turned around. The worldwide Christianity of which they spoke would come about, but as it emerged it would rebuff the norms of Western Christianity (or Christendom) and would consequently look different from Western Christianity. With the emergence of world Christianity, many new expressions of Christianity – Nigerian, Ghanaian, Zimbabwean, Brazilian, Jamaican, Korean, Indonesian, and many others – would rise. It is, of course, not sufficient to talk about national Christianity, because even in one country there will be different expressions of Christianity, usually distinct to tribal identities. Malawian Christianity, for instance, includes Chewa, Ngoni, Tumbuka, Lhomwe, Sena and Yao identities, to mention just a few. These different forms of localized Christianity emerge as a result of the contextualization of the faith as the gospel encounters various cultures around the world, and are a normative part of the faith itself. They ought to be understood as such. They will shape the multicultural encounters of Christians from different parts of the world. The cultural diversity that we see in British Christianity today exists because of these different expressions of the faith that have found their way to Britain, especially in the past 70 years. Indeed, among the Malawian Christian community in Britain, all these tribes are represented.

The empire strikes back

From the mid-1940s onwards – soon after the end of World War Two – political colonialism became difficult to sustain. Europe had been distracted by the war and anti-colonial movements had gained momentum in Africa and Asia. In 1947, India and Pakistan became independent nations. The European colonial empires that had spread their domination across the world would soon lose their colonies. They would bring home their colonial agents, while other Europeans returned because they did not feel safe in the colonies once the colonial governments lost power. Before long, the migration trends that had moved millions of Europeans and North Americans to the rest of the world slowed and came to a halt, and to some extent began to reverse. The world of the second half of the twentieth century made this both possible and necessary, for several reasons. First, returning Europeans from the colonies started to reverse the migration pattern that had been in place for centuries. Second, Europe needed to import labour after losing a generation of young people in the war. Britain, for instance, invited young men and women from the West Indies to migrate and work here. Third, life in the now independent colonies caused even more people to want to migrate to Europe, for reasons such as education or to escape from political instability. The liberation of the colonies ushered in a new wave of African (religious) migrants – diplomats, students and tourists – to Europe.

Thus, the brief era of the European colonization of Africa and parts of Asia has had a great but probably unforeseen consequence: making possible the migration of the colonized to the homelands of the colonizers. Immediately after gaining independence, citizens of the former colonies began to migrate to the countries of their former colonizers. Citizens of Anglophone Africa, for instance, naturally began to make their way to Britain: Nigerians, Ghanaians, Kenyans, and of course Indians. Similarly, citizens of Francophone Africa – Cameroon, Mali, Senegal – migrated to France. In the early days it was a trickle, mainly of officials of the newly formed governments who came for further education. Before long, and particularly in the case of Africa, people started to migrate when it became apparent that the independent nation states would struggle to succeed. By the 1970s, Africans and Asians were beginning to show up in large numbers in Western cities, wherever they had opportunities. It did not matter any more where people migrated to, as long as they made it to the West. Western governments responded by adapting their migration laws as and when needed, but the 'problem' of migration continued to cause them concern. However, migration continues to happen at an increasing pace. As they migrate, people bring with them their religions. By the end of the twentieth century, the religions of the colonial subjects – Hinduism, Buddhism, Islam, even African traditional religion – had begun to establish themselves in the Western world.

In the case of Britain, foreign Christianities have been around for most of the twentieth century. As early as 1906, a Ghanaian man by the name of Kwame Brem-Wilson (1855–1929) founded the Sumner Road Chapel in Peckham, London.[10] Later on, in 1931, Daniels Ekarte (1890s–1964), a Nigerian, founded the African Churches Missions in Toxteth, Liverpool.[11] The Windrush era brought many Christians from the West Indies to Britain, beginning in 1948 and continuing until the 1960s, by which time African migrants, especially from Anglophone West Africa, started to arrive. As a result, African churches had begun to mushroom across the country. By the 1980s, they started to institutionalize into formal denominations even though they maintained their headquarters in Africa.

Today, more than 70 years after the beginning of the Windrush migration of West Indians to Britain, Christians from different parts of the world now live, work and worship together in the cities of Britain. World Christianity is here in Britain. We see it in the many foreign expressions of faith coexisting, on high streets and in the suburbs. Temple and

Latourette had no means of knowing that Western religious hegemony would be strongly resisted by the rest of the world and that the colonial era would come to an abrupt end. When they celebrated the arrival of global Christianity, it was inconceivable that Christendom would be rejected by the non-Western world. (Eventually, of course, it would also be rejected by their fellow Europeans who favour secularism in place of Christianity.) It was unimaginable at the time that Europe would secularize so massively and so rapidly, precipitating the need for non-Western Christians to come and help evangelize the West. Back in the 1940s, it was almost impossible to imagine that Nigeria, for instance, would have more Anglicans by 2020 than Europe and North America put together. It was also beyond the realms of possibility that Nigerian Anglicans, like Bankole, would come to buttress the Church of England in London in just two generations.

Blessed reflex

One major contributing factor in the shaping of the worldwide kingdom of God is the work of William Carey in the years leading up to 1800. Carey was a Baptist minister born in 1761 near Kettering. In 1792 he published an essay entitled *An Enquiry into the Obligations of Christians to Use Means for the Conversion of the Heathens in which the Religious State of the Different Nations of the World, the Success of Former Undertakings, and the Practicability of Further Undertakings are Considered*.[12] He had spent quite some time collecting data about the religious state of different nations, which would serve as evidence for his argument that the world out there needed to hear the gospel, and that the English (or European) Christians had to take the gospel to them. Carey made a rudimentary map of the world showing populations of different parts of the world and their religions. He showed that there were many 'Mohammedans' and 'pagans' in Africa and Asia who needed Europeans to go and preach to them. He effectively proposed that (1) Europeans had the responsibility to preach to the nations, and (2) a few Christians could easily form an association that could then send and support missionaries to the un-evangelized world. Essentially, he convinced his audience that everybody, especially lay members of the Church, could get involved in mission.

Also in 1792, Carey formed the Baptist Missionary Society as a model for the outworking of his argument in the *Enquiry* and as a demonstration of his own conviction and commitment to mission. In 1793 he left England to become a missionary in India, where he served until his death in 1834 without ever returning to England. These three events – the publishing of the *Enquiry*, the formation of the Baptist Missionary Society, and Carey's going to serve in India – mark a tipping point in the story of world mission and Christianity. Carey's impact on world mission is so fundamental that he is often recognized as the father of modern missions. Indeed, it is impossible to tell of God's mission in the world, especially in the past two centuries, without acknowledging the towering influence of William Carey.[13] The world Christianity that we celebrate today has come about because of Carey's daring spirit. He is remembered for his bold statement: 'Expect great things from God; attempt great things for God.'

In the decades following 1792, the Protestant missionary movement gained great momentum. William Carey's work had opened the way. At the time, less than 10 per cent of world Christians lived outside the West. Yet, as Western missionaries went to evangelize the world (long before the colonial project), even then some spoke hopefully of the day when Christians from those unevangelized lands would come to help invigorate Western Christianity. They hoped for a day in the future when Christianity would grow so strong in Africa and Asia that African and Asian Christians would come to the West to strengthen Western Christianity. They called this phenomenon the 'blessed reflex'.[14] In understanding it as a 'reflex' they believed that it would happen naturally. Those being converted to Christianity in Latin America, Africa and Asia would themselves become missionaries, and would someday come to Europe. At that time in the history of Christianity, however, anticipating that some of the people converting to Christianity in Africa or Asia would engage in mission in the very countries that sent them missionaries, even if in theory only, was rather too ambitious. On the one hand, the transatlantic slave trade was yet to be abolished (although this happened in 1806, slave traders still pillaged Africa well into the 1880s and 1890s), so for many Europeans, black and brown peoples of the world were generally yet to be accepted as fully human. On the other, there was no indication that Christianity would thrive in Africa or in Asia. Even a hundred years later, in the early 1900s, there was no guarantee that Christianity would explode around the world as much as it has done. This optimism is hard to justify and, of course, it precedes (and was to be made futile by) much of the colonial expansion of Europe and the dehumanizing of Africans and Asians beyond Western civilization.

Nevertheless, and against all odds, at the beginning of the nineteenth century British Christians expected that the blessed reflex would happen. They looked forward to the day when Christians from lands like Africa and Asia would come to be part of the Christian presence in the West, and thereby strengthen its witness in Europe and North America. It is not clear how they envisaged this happening. If Carey's language is anything to go by, European attitudes towards Africans and Asians were extremely imperialistic and condescending. Carey referred to the millions of uncivilized 'pagans' and 'Mohammedans', reflecting the paternalistic tones with which Western Christians spoke of the rest of the world at the time. Of course, these attitudes would later justify Europe's colonizing of Africa, and they are even today prevalent in Europe's relationship with Africa. Regardless, Carey's followers still expected the same uncivilized black and brown Christians to invigorate Western Christianity. It would have taken a miracle in the pre-colonial world of the early 1800s for this to happen. What did they mean by 'invigorating'? Would it be just their numerical presence? How would they integrate into the wider European Christian landscape? How would they contribute to European Christianity? How would they theologize or worship? And one wonders why, at the time, they even thought that Western Christianity could ever get to a point of needing invigorating from foreign Christians.

Talk about the blessed reflex undergirded the hope that the lives of the many missionaries that were lost while working in the heathen lands were not being lost in vain. This, also, was its basis – should a time come in the future when European Christianity needed to be strengthened, Christians from other parts of the world would be able to help. Missionaries like William Carey in India and Johannes Rebmann in East Africa endured long years in the mission field and managed to catch a glimpse of the potential impact of their work. Others, like David Livingstone in Central Africa, saw only small breakthroughs in converting locals to the faith but nevertheless contributed strongly to mission through geographical exploration. (Livingstone is said to have converted only one person, who did not stay in the faith for long.) Whatever their work, it was not until the end of World War Two that the light of world Christianity began to rise on a distant horizon. Overall, the growing presence of non-Western Christians in Britain is a fruit of the work of the many sons and daughters of Britain, Europe and North America who went to be missionaries in other parts of the world: people like William Carey, Robert Moffatt, James Hudson Taylor, Charles McKenzie, Mary Slessor, Gladys May Aylward and many others.

Today, 200 years after that discourse, and on the other side of the colonial era, the blessed reflex is finally here. While the concept of the blessed reflex was unrealistic at the time, it has remained a subtext in mission history for two centuries. The prophetic seeds of that hope never died. The world Christianity that we see today is, to a large extent, the result of the work of the missionary movement of the nineteenth century. Numerous non-Western Christians from all over the world are living in Western cities. These world Christians in Europe, North America,

Australia and New Zealand are, in a sense, spiritual descendants of those early Western missionaries. This is the blessed reflex. It will help British Christians to appreciate that the African and Asian Christians who have made Britain their home are actually a fruit of the work of their ancestors. With such a small attitude change, it becomes possible for people to be grateful of one another's presence. Migrant Christians ought to be thankful for the British missionaries who went overseas for service. British Christians could also show gratitude for the fruit of their sacrifices that has come back to strengthen their own work in Britain today.

Looking back at the twentieth century

On a global scale, this emergence of world Christianity changes everything. It is evident that Christianity is fast becoming the non-Western religion that it once was.[15] This would never have been predicted at the turn of the twentieth century, when more than 80 per cent of Christians in the world lived in the West (Europe and North America in addition to their descendants in Australia and New Zealand), with a large part of the remaining 20 per cent of Christians being Western migrants (colonial agents, traders and missionaries) who had made their home outside the West. Almost 85 per cent of world Christians in 1910 were white, and were living in the Western world or in Western colonies, with a small number of them being Western missionaries to the unevangelized world.

To put this into perspective, let us talk about the landscape of Christianity in the world at the beginning of the twentieth century. One great snapshot we have of the time is the World Missionary Conference that took place in Edinburgh in June of 1910. When the missionaries came together from various parts of the world on 14 June it was a thoroughly Western affair. The conference attracted 1,215 delegates, of whom 509 came from Britain, 491 from North America, 169 from Continental Europe, 27 from the white colonies of South Africa and Australasia, and 19 were from the majority world (18 of these from Asia).[16] According to official records not one black African was in attendance.[17] Africa was represented by white missionaries. Black Africans were not invited because, as they said, 'the inhabitants of the African continent were widely regarded even by Christians as primitive, childlike, and at the bottom of the evolutionary hierarchy'.[18] Even though Asians were in attendance, they were not treated as full delegates. However, Brian Stanley also observes that there were none present at Edinburgh 'from the Christian communities of the Pacific Islands or the Caribbean, or any representative of the North American missionary presence in Latin America, or from the tribal peoples of the Southeast Asia, some of whom already had significant and rapidly growing Christian communities'.[19]

The conference itself was characterized by great optimism that their generation could evangelize the world in their lifetime.[20] As a matter of fact, this was the motto of the conference: 'to evangelize the world in this generation'. This had been the motto of the Student Volunteers Missionary Movement from the late 1800s and it seemed both convincing and doable enough for the Edinburgh 1910 conference organizers to adopt it as their motto too. Such was their desire and passion that they believed that the world would be won to Christ in their generation. John Mott, an American and one of the main organizers of the conference, was adamant that Edinburgh 1910 was 'a decisive hour for Christian missions' after which the world would never be the same.[21] What they understood as evangelizing the world is not clear, especially as the first decade of the twentieth century was also one of great colonial activity. Nevertheless, they were confident that the conference would precipitate the beginnings of the conversion of the world to Christianity. When they left Edinburgh, they were charged up to take the world for Christ. Little did they know that only four years later European *Christian* nations (Europe being Christendom or Christianity on the map) would engage each other in the war, and drag many other nations around the world into it too. The same Christian countries that hoped to evangelize the world in their generation were fighting one another. Their missionaries were interning one another in Kenya, Tanzania, South Africa and India, and in the process confusing the very people they sought to convert. The energy of the Edinburgh Conference would be washed away in the trenches in France. The world wondered whether Christianity, as proclaimed by the missionaries, was worth the hype if it could not prevent a European war.

It seems that neither at Edinburgh 1910 nor at any point in the first half of the twentieth century was there any anticipation that world Christianity would happen as fast as it did, and that when it happened it would look, feel and think very differently from the Christianity that was brought from the West through the work of the missionaries. They were confident that whatever Christianity would emerge in the world would look like what they were exporting from the West. Where forms of Christianity developed that did not look like Western Christianity, labels such as African Independent Churches were applied to demarcate them from their own work. Leaders of such independent churches often experienced a great deal of opposition from the colonial governments (who in some cases acted at the request of Western missionaries, who did not appreciate the un-Western nature of their churches). Both

William Wade Harris (of Liberia) and Simeon Kimbangu (of the Congo) were jailed with the aim of diminishing the impact of their ministries. In Malawi, for example, the colonial government passed a law that disallowed Malawians from leading national churches. That honour was reserved for white missionaries (including white Zimbabweans and South Africans).[22]

Soon after World War Two, the colonial empires started to lose hold. Pakistan and India became independent nations in 1947. China expelled all Western missionaries in the early 1950s. The following 20 years would see all but a few colonies gain independence, including almost all of Europe's sub-Saharan Africa. The rejection of political colonialism was also, in the case of sub-Saharan Africa, a rejection of the Western missionaries. The struggle to end political colonialism became a struggle to decolonize Christianity. Mission and colonialism had worked hand in hand for decades; it would not be possible for one to continue well without the other. The history of anti-colonial struggles in Africa is made up of stories of mission-school-educated African leaders who campaigned strongly (and often violently) for independence. In most African countries, European missionaries were responsible for education during the colonial era. Robert Mugabe of Zimbabwe is one example among many of Africans educated by missionaries who would later fight for the freedom of their countries.

More than 50 years after the Edinburgh 1910 conference, the emerging churches of the majority world (wrongly labelled 'younger churches') started to agitate for independence for their countries both from colonial rule and from Western missionaries in favour of indigenous Christian leadership in their countries. The decolonization of African Christianity took longer than that of the states, and some would say was a lot harder. In the view of most missionaries and their sending agencies, indigenous African leaders were not ready to take over leadership roles in their churches. However, the indigenous leaders themselves felt that they had matured enough to run their own affairs and did not need the missionaries to keep on guiding them. In Kenya, John Gatu, General Secretary of the Presbyterian Church of East Africa in the late 1960s, reports that the younger people pushed back against the missionaries' desires to stay on, saying: 'the Church is colonial and irrelevant, and we are not ready to stand the presence of foreign missionaries'.[23] By the 1960s, indigenous leaders were arguing for the decolonization of the missionary churches both in sub-Saharan Africa and in the wider non-Western world. 'Missionaries, go home!' became the rallying cry, as many wanted to be free from missionary influence.[24] It is largely because of these instances of resistance that world Christianity emerges and looks different in one part of the world from another, appearing nothing like the Christianity that came with the missionaries from Europe and North America.

Gatu proposed that there be a moratorium on Western churches sending missionaries to Africa. Gatu shocked the world when he suggested at a mission festival in Milwaukee, Wisconsin, USA in 1971 that neither Western missionaries nor Western money should be sent to African churches for at least five years. He went on to suggest a (permanent) withdrawal of all Western missionaries from Africa.

> The time has come for the withdrawal of the foreign missionaries from many parts of the Third World, that the churches of the Third World must be allowed to find their own identity and that the continuation of the present missionary movement is a hindrance to this selfhood of the church.[25]

He adds:

> We must ask missionaries to leave ... I started by saying that the missionaries should be withdrawn from the Third World for a period of at least five years. I will go further and say that the missionaries should be withdrawn, period.[26]

The moratorium debate lasted five years. It was met with fierce resistance from the West. Gatu was briefly labelled a heretic and consequently many Africans also withheld their support. As a result, it never came into effect. At the All Africa Council of Churches in Lusaka in 1974, Burgess Carr declared:

> To enable the African Church to achieve the power of being a true instrument of liberating and reconciling the African people, as well as finding solutions to economic and social dependency, our option as a matter of policy has to be a moratorium on external assistance in money and personnel. We recommend this option as the only potent means of becoming truly and authentically ourselves while remaining a respected and responsible part of the Universal Church.[27]

Yet the debate helped start conversations among majority world Christians about the nature of their own local Christianities. It also began a dialogue on whether cross-cultural mission is biblically mandated only for Westerners. Many began to wonder if they could engage in mission just like the Western missionaries who had worked among them. If the Church is indeed missionary by its very nature, as had been suggested by post-Willingen mission theologies,[28] were African and Asian churches also missionary by nature? Were Christians from the majority world churches also mandated to be missionaries, both in their own world and in the West? Though Gatu was not successful with the moratorium, the conversation he started eventually helped prepare the way for the rising of missionary movements among non-Western nations. It helped the concept of non-Western missionary movements take shape, grounding its rationale and determining its characteristics.

2010 World Mission Conferences

At Edinburgh 1910, there was a general feeling that Africa would continue to convert to Islam, partly because of the long-established Islam in North Africa. Commission 1 of the conference debated 'Carrying the Gospel to All the Non-Christian World' and in its report suggested that 'the ubiquitous and rapid advance of Islam is the great challenge to urgency in the evangelisation of Africa'.[29] Faced with this possibility, it was believed that Islam would win Africa. As a result, the mission leaders of the time committed their most promising missionaries to Asia and not Africa. Sub-Saharan Africa had fewer than 9 million Christians then (which incidentally was also the number of Muslims on the continent). Today, Africa has more than 630 million Christians. Christianity has grown well beyond any projections, and this has been the case not only in Africa but also in Latin America and some parts of Asia.

In 2010 there were several centennial celebrations of the Edinburgh 1910 conference. Major conferences took place in Edinburgh, Tokyo, Cape Town and Boston in 2010 and in San Jose in 2012. The 2010 conferences were remarkably different from Edinburgh 1910. Both the demographic make-up of the participants and the tone of the conversations reflected the reality that, somewhere between 1910 and 2010, world Christianity had emerged, and the percentage of Christians in the majority world had grown from less than 20 per cent to almost 70 per cent. The organizers of the 2010 conferences set out to reflect this new global nature of Christianity. Non-Western Christians were especially encouraged to attend and consequently the conferences of 2010 had more non-Western than Western delegates.

Edinburgh 2010 limited participation to only three hundred delegates (citing financial problems). These 300 delegates came from 202 mission agencies and represented 115 denominations, 75 nationalities and 61 different mother tongues. There were 41 delegates from the whole of Africa while the US had 45 and Britain had 35. Cape Town 2010 had 4200 evangelical leaders from 198 countries, and extended to hundreds of thousands more, participating in meetings around the world on-line. Tokyo 2010 had 967 delegates, 75 percent of these came from non-Western countries, representing 73 countries and 404 mission agencies were represented. Boston 2010 also had 300 delegates and three quarters of them were from the Majority World.[30]

World Christianity has emerged, but in my estimation not as a direct result of Edinburgh 1910. Today many of these non-Western expressions of Christianity are here in the West. Any major city in Europe and North America will have a good number of African, Asian and Latin American Christians.[32] Their presence has created a cultural diversity within Western Christian communities that has never existed before. As with anything new, it will take some time to figure out how these Christians from different parts of the world, with different cultures and theological traditions, can be the body of Christ together in one country.

Notes

1 Jehu Hanciles, *Beyond Christendom: Globalization, African Migration, and the Transformation of the West* (Maryknoll, NY: Orbis, 2008).

2 Afeosemime U. Adogame, *The African Christian Diaspora: New Currents and Emerging Trends in World Christianity* (London: Bloomsbury Academic, 2013).

3 Sheila Akomiah-Conteh, 'Church Growth in Scotland between 2000 and 2015', PhD dissertation, Aberdeen University, 2019.

4 Peter W. Brierley, *London's Churches are Growing! What the London Church Census Reveals* (Tonbridge: ADBC Publishers, 2013).

5 Brierley, *London's Churches are Growing!*

6 Peter W. Brierley, *Pulling Out of the Nose Dive: A Contemporary Picture of Church Going: What the 2005 English Church Census Reveals* (Tonbridge: ADBC Publishers, 2006).

7 William Temple, *The Church Looks Forward* (New York: Macmillan, 1944), p. 2.

8 Kenneth Scott Latourette, *The Emergence of a World Christian Community* (New Haven: Yale University Press, 1949).

9 Temple, *The Church Looks Forward*, p. 2.

10 Israel O. Olofinjana, 'The Significance of Multicultural Churches in Britain: A Case Study of Crofton Park Baptist Church', in R. Drew Smith, William Ackah and Anthony G. Reddie (eds), *Churches, Blackness, and Contested Multicultural-ism: Europe, Africa, and North America* (New York: Palgrave Macmillan, 2014), p. 80.

11 Marika Sherwood, *Pastor Daniels Ekarte and the African Churches Mission, Liverpool, 1931–1964* (London: Savannah Press, 1994).

12 It has been through many editions over the decades, and various versions of the essay are accessible online. While the world today is different from that of the

1780s, some of what William Carey says can still speak to us today. See William Carey, *An Enquiry into the Obligations of Christians to Use Means for the Conversion of the Heathens* (London: Carey Kingsgate, 1961).

13 Carey was himself influenced by the Moravians who had been sending missionaries to some parts of the world since the beginning of their revival in the 1730s. The Moravians also had an impact on John Wesley when he travelled with some of their missionaries on a trip to America in the 1740s.

14 See Kenneth R. Ross, '"Blessed Reflex" : Mission as God's Spiral of Renewal', *International Bulletin of Missionary Research* 27, no. 4 (2003).

15 For more on this argument, see Kwame Bediako, *Christianity in Africa: The Renewal of a Non-Western Religion* (Maryknoll, NY: Orbis, 1995).

16 Brian Stanley, *The World Missionary Conference, Edinburgh 1910*, Studies in the History of Christian Missions (Grand Rapids, MI: Eerdmans, 2009), p. 12.

17 Stanley says he later discovered that there was indeed one black man from Ghana, but he was not a delegate at the conference.

18 Stanley, *The World Missionary Conference, Edinburgh 1910*, p. 13.

19 Stanley, *The World Missionary Conference, Edinburgh 1910*.

20 John R. Mott, *The Evangelization of the World in this Generation* (New York: Student Volunteer Movement for Foreign Missions, 1900).

21 Stanley, *The World Missionary Conference, Edinburgh 1910*, p. 14.

22 Ulf Strohbehn, *Pentecostalism in Malawi: A History of the Apostolic Faith Mission in Malawi, 1931–1994*, Kachere theses (Zomba, Malawi: Kachere Series, 2005).

23 John Gatu, *Joyfully Christian and Truly African* (Nairobi: Acton, 2006), pp. 107–8. He is saying this in response to Stephen Neill who had argued that it was the older people who did not want the missionaries to stick around.

24 See Emele Mba Uka, *Missionaries Go Home? A Sociological Interpretation of an African Response to Christian Missions* (New York: Lang, 1989).

25 Bengt Sundkler and Christopher Steed, *A History of the Church in Africa*, Studia Missionalia Upsaliensia 74 (New York: Cambridge University Press, 2000), p. 1027.

26 R. Elliott Kendall, *The End of an Era: Africa and the Missionary* (London: SPCK, 1978).

27 Adrian Hastings, *A History of African Christianity, 1950–1975*, African Studies Series 26 (Cambridge: Cambridge University Press, 1979), p. 225.

28 David J. Bosch, *Transforming Mission: Paradigm Shifts in Theology of Mission*, American Society of Missiology Series (Maryknoll, NY: Orbis, 1991).

29 Oliphant, Anderson and Ferrier, *World Missionary Conference, 1910. Report of Commission One: Carrying the Gospel to All the Non-Christian World* (Edinburgh, 1910), p. 207.

30 Harvey C. Kwiyani, 'Mission in the Global South', in Cathy Ross and Colin Graham Smith (eds), *Missional Conversations: A Dialogue between Theory and Praxis in World Mission* (London: SCM Press, 2018).

31 A quick survey of this subject of non-Western Christians in the West will highlight such books as Rebecca Y. Kim, *The Spirit Moves West: Korean Missionaries in America* (Oxford: Oxford University Press, 2015). Also Harvey C. Kwiyani, *Sent Forth: African Missionary Work in the West*, American Society of Missiology Series (Maryknoll, NY: Orbis, 2014). In addition, Gastón Espinosa, *Latino Pentecostals in America: Faith and Politics in Action* (Cambridge, MA: Harvard University Press, 2014).

3

Shaping the Kingdom

The phenomenon of world Christianity is new. And it seems to have taken many by surprise. A hundred years ago it was not imaginable, nor was it expected. The missionaries who went to the unevangelized nations in the nineteenth century, wanting to evangelize the world 'in our generation' and believing the entire world could be evangelized in the early twentieth century, did not foresee world Christianity emerging the way it did. Until only a few decades ago, Christianity was still largely captive to the Western civilization and identity while Christian mission was used to push Western agendas to the rest of the world.

It was another 50 years after Edinburgh 1910 before world Christianity emerged, long after the powerful missionary movement of the early 1900s had lost both its footing and its confidence. Indeed, twentieth-century mission history seems to suggest that the Western missionary movement never regained its impetus after Edinburgh. It appears that Edinburgh was the watershed moment in the story of the Western missionary movement that had started with William Carey in 1792. Several conferences followed – Jerusalem (1928), Tambaram (1938), Canada (1948), Willingen (1952), Ghana (1958) – but the energy of 1910 was not there any more. In addition to the folly of two world wars and how they affected the Christian witness of the West in the world, the Western missionary movement's close relationship with European colonialism in Africa and Asia would lead to its eventual decline. By the mid-twentieth century, the world was rejecting the Western missionary movement largely because mission and colonialism seemed to most people to be two sides of the same coin: the missionaries and the colonial agents were partners in the European endeavour to dominate the world. The missionaries often depended on colonial agents for security while the colonizers would use the missionaries as peace brokers with local people. Western missionaries did more than just spread Christianity. Consequently, when the struggle against colonialism began, it would inevitably affect the missionaries. The Western missionary movement had associated itself too closely with the Western imperial project, and that was its end. I wonder, looking back at the nineteenth century, whether colonialism was an unavoidable consequence of the motive of the missionary movement as a whole, which could be summed up in commerce, civilization and Christianization. If colonialism is indeed a direct outcome of mission, which as mentioned earlier also benefited from the help of the colonial governments, how then do we talk about mission in a post-colonial world, in a global village where Christians are present in all nations and tribes?

In Africa, as in Asia, the withdrawal of the missionaries allowed for local forms of Christianity to emerge, with an indigenous leadership. The miraculous growth of Christianity in Africa is well documented. It has become something of a fascination in academic circles discussing world Christianity. The work of David Barrett and Todd Johnson continues to highlight the pace at which African Christianity is growing and how it is beginning to shape the global landscape of Christianity. Andrew Walls was right when he said, 'if you want to know something about Christianity today, you must know something about Africa'.[1] There is no way we can talk about world Christianity without at least acknowledging that the statistical centre of gravity of Christianity has rapidly shifted southwards to Africa. Africa is now the continent with the largest number of Christians, and African Christianity is slowly beginning to take centre stage in the discourse on world Christianity. Walls is also right when he says that a great deal of Christianity today is being shaped by events happening in places like Africa.

Beginning in the 1970s when Reinhard Bonnke's evangelistic campaigns (strangely called 'crusades') started to make waves, the world gradually became aware of the hundreds of thousands of people who were converting to Christianity every year. It was becoming clear that Africa would become the new Christian heartland. By the turn of the century, African Christianity had reached a critical mass that it could continue to grow biologically even if there were no new conversions. Having grown from 140 million to 650 million in 50 years, Africa has gained more than 10 million new Christians every year since 1970. That is more than the population of Switzerland, Austria or Sweden converting to Christianity every year for the last 50 years. Today, when we hear about the RCCG's Holy Ghost Convention, which gathers more than 2 million Christians in one place in Nigeria for prayers, it is not news any more. Shepherd Bushiri's crossover services in Tshwane, South Africa, gather around 100,000 Christians in a football stadium for worship. Even here in Britain, the RCCG's Festival of Life gathers more than 50,000 Christians for overnight prayers in London twice a year.

The story of Chinese Christianity is still largely underground, like most of Chinese Christianity itself. However, it is normal nowadays to hear of many millions of Christians in China; it is no secret that the Chinese Church is growing. Western missionaries were all expelled from the country in the early 1950s, but Mark Noll, commenting on the growth of Christianity in China, observes that 'forcing the missionaries to leave [China] was the birth of Christian China'. He adds: 'Even though there was tremendous suffering and momentous persecution, what was left was Chinese Christianity, and Chinese Christians knew how to do the gospel in China without the missionaries', before concluding that, 'In a strange way, losing China was how the gospel took root in China.'[2] Philip Jenkins writes that, 'Current estimates of Chinese Christian numbers vary enormously, from 25 million or so, to an incredible 200 million.'[3] The PEW Research Centre's Forum on Religion and Public Life suggested in 2010 there were more than 58 million Protestants in China.[4] Scholars of world religions agree that China will soon be among the countries with the most Christians. Jenkins suggests that China's total Christian population, including Catholics, will exceed 247 million before 2030, placing it above Mexico, Brazil and the United States as the largest Christian congregation in the world. Fenggang Yang, a Chinese professor of sociology at Purdue University, adds that 'China is destined to become the largest Christian country in the world very soon'.[5]

Both the African and the Chinese stories show that it is only in the second half of the twentieth century – after the missionaries had left Africa and Asia, placing the so-called 'young churches' under indigenous leadership – that Christianity became a worldwide religion. The work of the Western missionaries planted the seeds of Christianity in the world and watered them as they germinated. However, the blossoming of world Christianity (and maybe at this point it makes more sense to talk about world *Christianities*) required neither their continued presence nor their guidance. It was not until after the collapse of the colonial empires of the nineteenth and twentieth centuries that indigenous Christian presence began to explode in many parts of the world. We know today that world Christianity flourishes best where it is able to express itself in indigenous ways, and missionaries are generally unable to make room for this to happen. Unfortunately, our missiology still believes that Christianity is only real if it is led by Westerners, and that is why we hear more about the decline of the Church in Europe and North America when we could be celebrating the growth of Christianity in other parts of the world.

people don't see it as a win if it's not them

Behold the new Christians

In a nutshell, then, Christianity has spread to all corners of the world in the past 50 to 70 years, in the lifetime of the boomer generation. Christianity was until the late twentieth century a religion of Europeans and their descendants in North America, Australia, New Zealand and the parts of the world they colonized. People who were born in the 1940s came into a world where more than 75 per cent of Christians were white and lived in the West. As recently as 1950, to be a Christian was, generally speaking, to be white, and to be white was also synonymous with being a Christian. Europe was still Christendom – the Christian region of the world. Being born white or European was to be born a Christian, and this had been the case for many centuries.

The coming of world Christianity begins to liberate Christianity from its centuries of Western captivity. It begins to change the image of Christianity. It has become commonplace to hear of the changing *face* of Christianity, or the browning or de-Europeanization of Christianity. World Christianity also begins to liberate the Church from its white identity. As we come to the end of the second decade of the twenty-first century, almost 70 per cent of Christians in the world are not white and they do not live in Europe or North America. To put this another way, only three out of every ten Christians in the world are white. If someone took a snapshot of all the Christians living in the world today – think of John's vision in Revelation 7 – white Christians would be a minority, and actually a shrinking minority. Latin America, Africa and Asia contain more than 65 per cent of world Christians, which means of course that most Christians in the world are black or brown. The average Christian in the world is darker in skin complexion than has been the case for the past millennium. We will do well to get used to the idea of Latin American, African and Asian Christians.

This is the new reality that shapes our religious landscape. 'Black and Christian' is the new normal, or as one Zimbabwean young prophetess in London once told me, 'black is the new Christian'. It should thus be normal now for us to think of African Christians, or Latin American Christians, or Asian Christians. The sharp rise in the numbers of world Christians now means that the typical image of a Christian is no longer a white middle-class college-educated European man living in Brussels, London, Paris or Rome, but rather a less affluent non-European woman, living in the slums of Lagos or Nairobi or a village in rural Brazil or Thailand. It should make sense then that Christianity is becoming not just a non-Western religion but also a non-white one.

Almost 50 per cent of Africa's population of 1.2 billion are Christians –

that is, 600 million *non-white* Christians. This means that it is likely that one in every two Africans that you will ever meet is a Christian. In more than a few countries in Africa over 90 per cent of the population identify as Christians. For instance, São Tomé and Príncipe has 97 per cent of its population of 200,000 identifying as Christians while Cape Verde has 95 per cent of its 540,000 inhabitants adhering to Christianity. In Burundi, it is suggested that up to 94 per cent of the population are Christians. In addition, there are countries that have very large populations with quite high percentages of Christians. For instance, the Democratic Republic of Congo has over 95 per cent of its 81 million inhabitants identifying as Christians. That is to say, there now exists over 73 million Christians in a country that had virtually no Christians a few generations ago. Nigeria has over 80 million Christians *in one country*. Overall, of Africa, Gina Zurlo and Todd Johnson[6] give us the following statistics from 2015:

Largest population of Christians

1 Nigeria: 84,133,000
2 Democratic Republic of Congo: 73,384,000
3 Ethiopia: 58,574,000
4 South Africa: 44,690,000
5 Kenya: 37,275,000
6 Uganda: 32,958,000
7 Tanzania: 29,584,000
8 Angola: 23,223,000
9 Ghana: 17,625,000
10 Mozambique: 14,818,000

Highest percentage of Christians

1 São Tomé and Príncipe: 96%
2 Democratic Republic of Congo: 95%
3 Cape Verde: 94.9%
4 Burundi: 93.4%
5 Angola: 92.8%
6 Lesotho: 92.1%
7 Rwanda: 91.5%
8 Namibia: 90.8
9 Congo: 89.3%
10 Swaziland: 88.3%

The Pew Research Centre projects that by 2060, six of the countries with the top ten largest Christian populations worldwide will be in Africa, and these will be:

1 Nigeria: 174,200,000
2 Democratic Republic of Congo: 160,000,000
3 Tanzania: 117,000,000
4 Uganda: 96,200,000
5 Kenya: 91,7000,000
6 Ethiopia: 87,600,000[7]

In addition to this changing complexion of Christianity, there is the massive shift in its physical geographical location. Less than 40 per cent of Christians in the world currently live in the West. A hundred years ago, 85 per cent of Christians lived in Europe and North America; even 50 years ago 85 per cent lived in the West. Since the 1970s, we have seen a huge shift. Many lands that were called 'unevangelized' in the nineteenth century have embraced Christianity. In 1900, Africa had no more than 9 million Christians, most of them in Egypt (Coptic Christians) and Ethiopia (of the Ethiopian Orthodox Church). These 9 million represented 9 per cent of Africa's population at the time and less than 1 per cent of Christians in the world. Fast forward 50 years, and those 9 million Christians had multiplied to about 100 million, most of them in African Independent Churches (for instance, the Harrist Church in West Africa and the Kimbanguist Church in the Congo) and were therefore independent from the influence of the missionaries. That figure continues to rise to about 150 million Christians in Africa in 1970, and to 500 million in 2000. At the time of writing in 2019, Africa has more than 650 million Christians, representing 30 per cent of world Christians. This explosive growth is unprecedented in the history of Christianity's 2,000 years. At 650 million, Africa has more Christians than Europe. Nigeria currently has more Anglicans than all the Anglicans in Europe and North America put together. This massive growth of Christianity in Africa and other parts of the world has made it possible for Christianity to maintain steadily at one third of world population. As it wanes in Europe and other parts of the West, it has become stronger in other parts of the world, in Latin America, Africa and parts of Asia.

As a result of this unshackling of Christianity from Europe and North America, the religious landscape of the world has been drastically transformed in various ways. Non-Western Christians around the world have continued to tremendously increase in number. Continents and countries that had little to no Christian presence a hundred years ago now boast significant Christian communities. Some even send missionaries not just to other non-Western countries but also to Europe and North America, to the very countries that sent them missionaries two centuries ago. Todd Johnson predicts that between now and 2050, Africa's Christian population will almost double. A time is not far away when Africa will have more than a billion Christians. When this happens, Africa will be home to 45 per cent of all Christians in the world.

Who is the heathen now?

As Christianity has exploded in the majority world, the number of Christians in the Western world has steadily decreased. Secularism – or secular humanism, as it has been called – has risen to displace religion in Europe, and its worst victim has been Christianity. Since the end of World War Two, the number of Europeans who self-identify as Christians has gone down drastically. There has been a cultural revolution in Europe that has made it easy – if not fashionable – for people to disassociate themselves from Christianity. The culture of most European countries, which was not too long ago Christian (though often only nominally), now refuses to accommodate any symbols of Christianity in the public sphere. Christians can lose their job for wearing symbols of their religion to work, or talking about faith to their clients. While Christians are leaving the Church in large numbers, the percentage of people identifying as non-religious has risen sharply – to somewhere between 50 and 80 per cent of the population in most European countries. Even the most religious of European countries, then, are likely to have at least half of their populations registering as non-religious. The British Social Survey of 2016 reported that 53 per cent of the British population is non-religious.[8] In North America the percentage would probably be lower, as it is a little more Christian than Europe – an American form of Christendom still exists – but Australia and New Zealand seem to be secularizing just as much as Europe.

As a result of this secularization, European churches have lost millions of members since the 1950s. Essentially, Europe has become a mission field. The countries that sent missionaries to other parts of the world in the past now need missionaries sent to them. These changes on the global Christian landscape have happened rather abruptly. My parents' generation, born in Malawi in the 1940s, have witnessed these changes first-hand. They were born into colonialism, two decades before Malawi would become independent. Malawi's population was less than 5 million and only a small percentage of them were Christians. European missionaries were still teaching Malawians why and how to be Christians. They were also running most of the education system in the country which at that time comprised a few mission primary and secondary schools – no tertiary education was yet available in the country. The missionaries also ran clinics and hospitals across the country. The general Malawian population was under the heavy-handed leadership of the British colonial government on the one side and European missionaries (mainly Scottish, Dutch and Anglican) and South African (Afrikaner), on the other. Both my father and my mother were born into Christian homes of staunch members of the Church of Central Africa Presbyterian (CCAP) – my father in Malawi, my mother in Zimbabwe.[9] The CCAP is the offspring of a rather strange amalgamation of the mission works of the Church of Scotland, the Free Church of Scotland and the Dutch Reformed Church Mission (of South Africa) – an African denomination based on a Scottish Presbyterian ecclesiology. It was active in Malawi, Zambia and Zimbabwe. Growing up, my parents saw the CCAP membership expand exponentially as both Malawi's population exploded (which meant many new Presbyterian Christians were born) and thousands of new converts joined. They also saw the CCAP learn to stand on its own feet after Malawi gained independence from Britain. (I learned much later that the decolonization of the CCAP from the missionaries' leadership was more difficult than the country's struggle against political colonialism in the country.) Today, 55 years after Malawi gained independence, Malawi's population has grown to 19 million, and 80 per cent of Malawians are Christians – that is a massive 15 million Christians in a country that had only a few hundred in 1900. Malawi has more Christians than twice the entire population of Scotland.

My father, who with my mother has led a church in Malawi for the past 30 years, is always keen to say that 'the change has been much bigger and much faster than we could ever anticipate, and we have not had time to reflect on it yet'. He is correct. Many of my European friends struggle to understand what this all means to them. They still do not know how to react to the fact that Europe is not at the centre of the Christian story any more. They do not understand that Europeans are a minority in the global body of Christ – that there are more black Christians than there are white Christians. Or that there are more Anglicans in Nigeria or Uganda than in England. Even though they are Christians, they do not know how to relate with fellow Christians from countries they used to colonize. Most do not understand that Europe is a mission field and needs a new missional engagement that should involve the majority world Christians helping to re-evangelize her. More than a few European Christians have told me that they find it difficult to believe that an African can be a missionary, let

why we preach missions is problematic

alone a missionary in Europe. The change has been too deep and too fast. There are currently more church-attending Anglicans in Nigeria alone than in Europe and North America put together. There are more Presbyterians in Malawi than in Europe. There are more Methodists in Ghana than in Britain. There are more Baptists in the Democratic Republic of Congo than in North America. Both Latin America and Africa have each more Christians than the old Christian heartland of Europe. Christianity today is indeed a non-Western religion.

What in the world is going on?

Numerous commentators are at work to help us make sense of this new reality. Todd Johnson of the Centre for the Study of World Christianity at Boston University tells us that Christianity's statistical centre of gravity has shifted significantly southwards in the past 100 years. It is no longer in Europe where it has been for most of the past 2,000 years. It is now in West Africa, somewhere in Mali, and slowly moving south to Nigeria, where it is likely to remain for the next few generations. With the help of a team of researchers, Johnson publishes yearly statistical data following the trends in the distribution of Christianity. His 2018 report surprised the world when it showed that Africa has surpassed Latin America and Europe to be the continent with the most Christians, much earlier than anticipated.[10] The report suggested that the decline of Christianity in Europe is much sharper than had been believed before; absolute numbers of Christians in Europe are in a nosedive.

Philip Jenkins warns us in his book *The Next Christendom: The Coming of Global Christianity* of the 'new Christendom' that is currently emerging in Latin America, Africa and Asia. Agreeing with Todd Johnson, Jenkins says:

> Over the past century, the centre of gravity in the Christian world has shifted inexorably southward, to Africa, Asia, and Latin America. Already today, the largest Christian communities on the planet are to be found in Africa and Latin America. If we want to visualize a 'typical' contemporary Christian, we should think of a woman living in a village in Nigeria or in a Brazilian favela.[11]

He adds:

> By 2050, only about one-fifth of the world's 3 billion Christians will be non-Hispanic Whites. Soon, the phrase 'a White Christian' may sound

like a curious oxymoron, as mildly surprising as 'a Swedish Buddhist'. Such people can exist, but a slight eccentricity is implied.[12]

Since Jenkins wrote *The Next Christendom* in 2002, the growth trends in world Christianity make him sound overly conservative. It is very likely that we will not have to wait until 2050 to see the percentage of white Christians in the world drop well below 30 per cent. This may well happen before 2030. His prediction that Africa might just become the most Christian continent by 2025 was way off the mark, as Africa overtook Europe and Latin America to have the highest percentage of Christians in 2018. In addition, I do not find Jenkins's book title helpful. What we see developing in the world is *not* the next Christendom; it is actually not Christendom at all. He does acknowledge that the term 'Christendom' is problematic, but it would be more appropriate to find another term that makes sense. Certainly, the European style of Christendom cannot be replicated in Africa, and it would be also hard to do so in Latin America. There are far too many differences in people's worldviews and cultures for Christendom to take root. For example, most of the majority world is comfortable with religious pluralism, which is often a problem in Europe and North America. However, overall, Jenkins makes a good point. Non-Western Christianity is on the rise as Western Christianity is losing ground. Against the outcry generally heard in European and American missiology that the Church is 'top-heavy' (meaning that churches are largely patronized by older people) and 'haemorrhaging' (losing members), Christianity on the global platform is alive and well, thriving and growing rapidly in Latin America, Africa and some parts of Asia. African Christianity is full of young people – the median age of African Christians is less than 20.

In 2009, John Micklethwaite and Adrian Wooldridge wrote a book entitled *God is Back* in which they argue strongly that, to the surprise of many Westerners, the secularization theories of the mid-twentieth century were greatly misplaced.[13] Religion has not disappeared, as the secularization scholars predicted. To the contrary, religion is back with a vengeance. On a global scale, people are becoming more religious. The authors agree with Peter Berger that the world has become furiously religious[14] at a time when Europe is becoming even more secular. They suggest that all over the world, the Christian God (especially the God of Pentecostal Christians) is back and stronger than ever. Thus, generally speaking, Christianity is growing in the world even though it is not growing in Europe and other Western contexts. Realistically speaking, contemporary Christianity is largely a non-Western religion which has its centres of numerical strength in Latin America, Africa and Asia.

Notes

1 Andrew F. Walls, 'Of Ivory Towers and Ashrams: Some Reflections on Theological Scholarship in Africa', *Journal of African Christian Thought* 3, no. 1 (2000).

2 Philip Jenkins, *The Next Christendom: The Coming of Global Christianity*, 3rd edn (New York: Oxford University Press, 2011), p. 87.

3 Jenkins, *The Next Christendom*, p. 88.

4 The PEW Forum on Religion and Public Life, *Global Christianity: A Report on the Size and Distribution of the World's Christian Population*, Pew Research Centre (Washington DC, 2011).

5 Tom Philips, 'China on course to become "world's most Christian nation" within 15 years', *The Telegraph* (London) 2014. See www.telegraph.co.uk/news/worldnews/asia/china/10776023/China-on-course-to-become-worlds-most-Christian-nation-within-15-years.html (accessed 23.8.19).

6 Gina Zurlo and Todd Johnson, 'Religious Demographies of Africa, 1970–2025', in Isabel Apawo Phiri et al. (eds), *Anthology of African Christianity* (Oxford: Regnum, 2016).

7 Jeff Diamant and The Pew Research Centre, *The Countries with the 10 Largest Christian Populations and the 10 Largest Muslim Populations*, www.pewresearch.org/fact-tank/2019/04/01/the-countries-with-the-10-largest-christian-populations-and-the-10-largest-muslim-populations/ (accessed 1.9.19).

8 NatCen Social Research, 'British Social Attitudes 34: Record Number of Brits with no Religion', http://natcen.ac.uk/news-media/press-releases/2017/september/british-social-attitudes-record-number-of-brits-with-no-religion/ (accessed 12.9.19).

9 The CCAP is the offspring of a rather strange amalgamation of the mission works of the Church of Scotland, the Free Church of Scotland and the Dutch Reformed Church Mission (of South Africa) – an African denomination based on a Scottish Presbyterian ecclesiology. Being, as it is called, the Church of Central Africa Presbyterian, it has dioceses in Malawi, Zambia and Zimbabwe.

10 Todd Johnson et al., 'Christianity 2018: More African Christians and Counting Martyrs', *International Bulletin of Mission Research* 42, no. 1 (2018).

11 Jenkins, *The Next Christendom*, p. 2.

12 Jenkins, *The Next Christendom*, p. 3.

13 John Micklethwaite and Adrian Wooldridge, *God is Back: How the Global Revival of Faith is Changing the World* (New York: Penguin, 2009).

14 Peter L. Berger, *The Desecularization of the World: Resurgent Religion and World Politics* (Grand Rapids, MI: Eerdmans, 1999), p. 2.

4

The Mission of the Kingdom

William Carey founded the Baptist Missionary Society in 1792. His publication, *The Enquiry*, and his exemplary missionary work in India began to convince British (and European) Protestant Christians that it was possible and desirable for small associations of mission-minded Christians to support missionaries in what was then the unevangelized world. His map of the religious landscape of the world at the time, in addition to his own missionary work in India (which was made possible through the support of the Baptist Missionary Society), proved to many that the call to mission was relevant to Protestant Christians, and it was possible to be involved without the big structures like the mendicant orders of the Catholic Church. Protestant denominations responded favourably, but it was largely through smaller associations of like-minded people who came together to form societies that harnessed Carey's momentum. Before long, several mission societies emerged in Europe and North America. The London Missionary Society (LMS) was formed in 1795, after William Carey, who was already in India, asked some friends to reiterate the need for missionaries to spread Christianity. The LMS would be made famous in the 1850s through the work of the Scottish missionary David Livingstone in southern Africa. The Church Missionary Society (CMS) was formed in 1799, coming into existence as a response to requests for missionaries in India. The first such request had come from Charles Grant and George Uday of the East India Company in 1787, six years before William Carey got to India (and probably influenced Carey's choice to go to India). Carey's arrival in India and his correspondence to friends in England would add urgency to the call. The CMS was formed by a group of the Clapham Sect, and William Wilberforce was among its founders. Its work, both in the struggle to abolish the slave trade and in mission in West Africa, still bears witness to the significance of the missionary movement of the 1800s and to William Carey's work.

In 1800, there was very little Christian presence outside the West. David Barrett informs us that there were 205 million Christians in the world in 1800 (22 per cent of the total global population of 904 million).[1] Of these, 172 million were in Europe and Russia, only 6 million were in

North America. Thus more than 85 per cent of Christians in the world lived in Europe and North America. Africa had 4.3 million Christians (2 per cent of world Christians) while Latin America had 15 million (7 per cent). In Africa, the Christian population was comprised mainly of the Coptic Church which was strong in Egypt and the Ethiopian Orthodox Church which was home to hundreds of thousands of Ethiopian Christians. Both these Christianities have been in existence for more than 1,600 years.[2] In addition, there was a small, powerful and growing number of European (mostly Dutch) Christians in South Africa. The Christian kingdom of the Kongo that had existed since the late 1400s had disappeared at this point. William Carey's data as shown in the *Enquiry*, rudimentary as it was, captured the essence of this reality. The majority of the world population were not Christian. Outside Europe and North America, Carey asserted that there were 'Papists, Jews, Mohammedans and Pagans'. Africa, as far as he could understand it at the time, was full of pagans with a few Christians and Jews, especially to the North. It is this data and language that made it possible for mission societies to recruit young men and women to give up home comforts for the sake of expanding the reach of Christianity in Africa and Asia.

The 30-year period from 1792, when William Carey and friends formed the Baptist Missionary Society, were decades of great missionary momentum, which escalated the rise of the Western Protestant missionary movement. By the time of Carey's death in India in 1834, many missionary societies had been formed both in Europe and North America, and thousands of European and North American missionaries had gone to serve God in Africa, Asia and the wider non-Western world where the unevangelized mission field was believed to be at the time. Essentially, William Carey mainstreamed mission for Protestant Christians, and in the process sensitized many Christians to mission. As a result of his initiative, Western missionaries travelled across the world to spread Christianity, often carrying their belongings in a coffin (in which they would be buried when they died on the mission field). This momentum continued until the early 1900s. It is largely due to Carey's influence that Kenneth Latourette would recognize the nineteenth century as the 'great century of mission'. The missionary movement that began as a small stream in 1792 became a mighty river before the end of the nineteenth century, making it seem as if the Western missionary movement could indeed convert the world in their generation. Mission was not only a way of obeying the great commission (Matt. 28.19); it was a way of civilizing the masses, and thus saving their souls from eternal damnation in eternal fire. It had to be done with a sense of urgency.

Mission from everywhere to everywhere

Fifty years after 1910, the world had changed greatly, after two world wars and the collapse of colonial empires. The percentage of Christians living outside Europe and North America had risen to something between 15 and 20 per cent. The Western missionary movement had begun to slow down and the colonial migrations of Europeans to the rest of the world was in reverse. In 1963, the first conference of the Commission for World Mission and Evangelism (CWME) – a congress under the World Council of Churches – took place in Mexico City under the theme 'Mission in Six Continents', and there people began to conceptualize the possibilities of mission as a six-continent affair.[3] There was a realization that mission in the post-colonial world context had to involve Christians in every continent and not only those evangelizing in the global South, and that missionaries could move from any continent to any other continent. Michael Goheen says that this understanding of mission:

> derives from the World Council of Churches ecumenical missionary conference in Mexico City in 1963, which enunciated its theme as 'witness in six continents'. If one considers mission from the standpoint of geography, then mission is not to three continents (Asia, Africa, Latin America) from two continents (Europe, North America). Rather, it is *from* all six continents, including Africa and Asia; it is *to* all six continents, including Europe and North America; and it is *in* all six continents. The whole of God's world is a mission field, and the 'base' for mission is in every congregation in every part of the world.[4]

The days of Western missionary dominance are over, not because there are no more Western missionaries, but because world Christianity is here, and world Christians have caught the vision of the missionary God and are engaged and energized. This new era of Christianity has serious implications for the way we engage in the mission of God in our world today. While in theory it makes sense for missionaries from any continent and country to serve and work in any other country or continent, in reality the idea of a non-Western missionary is still new to many. Nevertheless, just as it is still commonplace for Western missionaries to serve in Asia, Africa and Latin America, it should be acceptable and expected that non-Western missionaries will work in the West. Indeed, it is something of a necessity since we live in a world where less than 40 per cent of Christians live in the West, there has been serious decline in Western Christianity since the 1960s, and many Western cities are home to migrants from other parts of the world and thus are best characterized by cultural diversity. The growth of Christianity in Latin America, Africa and Asia has resulted in the emergence of new missionary movements outside the Western world. Many of their missionaries serve in other majority world countries but some of them have migrated to the West.

It is especially the Evangelical and the Pentecostal/Charismatic branches of Christianity that have exploded around the world, particularly since the collapse of the colonial empires in the 1960s. These branches of Christianity encourage their members to evangelize to help people become born again in order to avoid hell. In many parts of Africa, this message has brought numerous people to conversion and then equipped and sent them out as evangelists and missionaries.

The Asian missionary movement

Several countries in Asia have seen a massive growth in Christianity in the twentieth century. South Korea is one of those countries. South Korea sends more missionaries per capita around the world than any other country except the United States. Their long-term missionaries can be found in many parts of the globe, and their presence in Africa is formidable. An article in the *New York Times* in 2004 states:

> The Koreans have joined their Western counterparts in more than 160 countries, from the Middle East to Africa, from Central to East Asia. Imbued with the fervor of the born again, they have become known for aggressively going to – and sometimes being expelled from – the hardest-to-evangelize corners of the world. Their actions are at odds with the foreign policy of South Korea's government, which is trying to rein them in here and elsewhere.[5]

It is the first time that large numbers of Christian missionaries have been deployed by a non-Western nation, one whose roots are Confucian and Buddhist, and whose population remains two-thirds non-Christian. Unlike Western missionaries, whose work dovetailed with the spread of colonialism, South Koreans come from a country with little history of sending people abroad until recently. They proselytize not in their own language but in the local one or English.

> 'There is a saying that when Koreans now arrive in a new place, they establish a church; the Chinese establish a restaurant; the Japanese, a factory', said a South Korean missionary in his 40's, who has worked here for several years and, like many others, asked not to be identified because of the dangers of proselytizing in Muslim countries.[6]

The African missionary movement

The continent of Africa is home to millions of displaced peoples, largely due to political conflicts, economic instability and poor living and health conditions. Many millions more have been displaced into what has come to be known as the 'African diaspora' – a collective name for Africans living outside Africa. A huge percentage of these have migrated to the West. The displacements have been so extensive that some scholars have suggested that Africa is the most displaced and therefore the most mobile continent. While Africans are migrating in all directions, the continent is also fast becoming a Christian stronghold. There are more than 10 million new conversions to Christianity taking place every year around the continent. Statistical projections suggest that by 2040, over 40 per cent of world Christians will live in Africa.

African migrations are both intra- and extra-continental. More Africans have migrated from one country to another within the continent than have migrated to other continents. In Africa, mission has been carried out mostly by Africans, both as a result of African Christians – rarely identifying themselves as missionaries – going to evangelize and proselytize people in other countries, and simply because of the migration of Christians from one country to another. It is a well-accepted fact that Africa has been evangelized by other Africans.[7]

In addition, the majority of African migrants who are spread around the world are Christians, and in migrating they bring their Christianity with them. Where they cannot join existing churches, they do not hesitate to form their own congregations. The Redeemed Christian Church (from Nigeria) can be found in more than 175 countries around the world (including almost every country in Africa). The Church of Pentecost (from Ghana) is found in 92 countries. The largest church in Europe, the Blessed Embassy of the Kingdom of God, located in Kiev, Ukraine, is led by a Nigerian known as Sunday Adelaja. Here in Britain, the largest church is the Kingsway International Christian Centre and it is led by another Nigerian, Matthew Ashimolowo.

West Indian Christian presence in Britain

Another aspect of African missionary work in Britain that must be acknowledged is that of the Afro-Caribbean Christians who have been present in England since the 1940s and 1950s. These are generally descendants of African people who were enslaved during the transatlantic slave trade and taken to the West Indies and the Americas several centuries ago. Their migration from 'The Islands' to Britain was accelerated in the 1950s when Caribbean families responded to an invitation from the British government to come and help rebuild the country after the devastation of the war. The first wave of these Afro-Caribbean immigrants is usually referred to as the Windrush generation, after the ship, SS *Empire Windrush*, that arrived with 493 people from the Caribbean on 22 June 1948 at Tilbury, London. The majority of the people from the Caribbean regarded themselves as British citizens, being part of the Commonwealth, and therefore expected to be treated as such. They soon realized that this was an illusion; the wealth was not common and they were second-class citizens. In their quest for survival, they turned to forming their own congregations. Today their presence is seen in Afro-Caribbean denominations like the Church of God of Prophecy and the New Testament Church of God. Both these denominations are in their second or third generation of existence. The flagship church for the Afro-Caribbean community in Britain today is the Ruach City Church in Brixton, London.[8]

The Latin American missionary movement

Latin American missionaries have also made their impact around the world. In England, some of the largest migrant congregations consist of members from Latin America. One of the many ministries dedicated to the livelihood of Spanish- and Portuguese-speaking Christians from Latin America in Britain – called Latin Link – seeks to help them reach British people with the gospel while at the same time encouraging a fraternity among them in the diaspora.

In the case of Roman Catholic Christianity in North America, Hispanics now account for one-third of all Catholics, largely due to massive Hispanic immigration from Latin America. And as long as current trends hold, Hispanic Christian presence in the Catholic Church in North America will continue to rise for the foreseeable future.[9] As Father Virgilio Elizondo has suggested in his widely acclaimed book *The Future is Mestizo*, to survive this generation the Roman Catholic Church in the United States must embrace the cultural diversity that has come about through the presence of Hispanic Catholics in the country.[10] Pentecostal Christianity in the United States has also been greatly invigorated by the presence of Hispanic Christians, mainly from Mexico. Hispanic Pentecostals form the second largest group of Latin Americans in the United States. Their numbers are growing rapidly and they are becoming increasingly powerful. The largest Assemblies of God church in the United States is the New Life Covenant Church in Chicago. Its 11,000-strong member-ship is largely Hispanic and the church is pastored by a Latino pastor, Wilfredo De Jesús.[11]

European migration and colonialism

Nineteenth-century history is usually dominated by the rise of Europe (and the Western civilization), best characterized by the industrial revolution, colonial expansion, and the migration of Europeans (or Euro-pean Christians) to the rest of the world. It was a European century, dominated by stories of how Europe appropriated the world to itself. Thus, Europe's relationship with the Americas, Africa and Asia in the nineteenth century shaped much of the world of the people then, and it shapes ours today. At the beginning of the nineteenth century, Europeans were curious to explore the land masses that were largely unknown to them, such as the interior of Africa. The Europeans wanted to know what was hiding inside the 'dark interiors' of the African continent.[12] They desired to find the source of the rivers they only saw on the coast, as the Niger, Congo, Zambezi, Nile, among others, entered the sea. They went in search of trade materials, including precious stones and spices (to further strengthen the industrial revolution). By the mid-nineteenth century, European explorers' travel journals had become accessible and popular with people at home, bringing information about foreign lands and peoples. Following on from the missionary momentum of the early decades of the century, Europeans became even more interested in Christianizing and civilizing the nations. Many missionaries followed.

However, it was not just mission – the movement of European mission-aries and Christians to extend Christianity to the unevangelized world – that occurred as a result of the early decades of European exploration of the world. If anything, mission ended up constituting a very small part of European presence in the majority world. Several other major develop-ments took place. In a nutshell, by the end of the nineteenth century more than 20 per cent of Europe's population had migrated to the rest of the world, for various reasons. At first they migrated for economic purposes. Europe was believed to be overpopulated at the time, and people were encouraged to migrate to take advantage of the world that was opening up to them. Soon they realized that there was a lot to be gained – espe-cially access to resources for the industrial revolution that would build European nations – and that to gain this they had to colonize those who were living there before their arrival. This naturally led to more Europe-ans migrating to the emerging colonies. Over the course of the nineteenth century, more than 60 million Europeans migrated from Europe to other parts of the world. Christian missionaries were involved in the exploration of the continents and in the colonizing of the nations, as well as the Christianizing of the people; a good example is David Livingstone, who worked for both the London Missionary Society and the Royal Geographical Society. He argued that Britain needed to have colonies in Africa, for such is a God-given right to Britain, and in the proposed British colony there would be no slave trade. His family later held colonial property in Central Africa; his grandson, Alexander Livingstone Bruce, lived in Malawi for quite some time, managing the family's estates at Magomero and Liwulezi.

Before any serious fruit of the European missionary efforts of the early 1800s began to register, Europe's attitudes and opinions about her relationship with Africa and Asia shifted from 'Christianize and civilize' to 'Christianize and colonize'. It was no longer enough to Christianize them and thereby set them free to be equal members of the Christian commonwealth. Europe had to colonize Africans, Indians, Asians and others, often justifying their acts by believing that it was for the good of those colonized. Influenced, I believe, by the slow demise of the transatlantic slave trade and the subsequent need for a new form of trade (mainly for Europe but for the Africans as well), and the somewhat successful European colonization in North America, European nations started to colonize parts of Africa and Asia, establishing European rule, grabbing land and other resources, often forcing local people to provide free labour (generally with little success). In 1858 large parts of India and what is now Pakistan were put under British rule. Two decades later, King Leopold II of Belgium began the process of acquiring the entire region of the Congo (current Democratic Republic of Congo) as his personal property, a landmass more than 70 times the size of Belgium at the time. In 1884, 14 European states gathered in Berlin, under the patronage of Otto von Bismarck, with the purpose of sharing the cake of Africa among themselves. They then spent the 1890s scrambling to establish their rule in the colonies, and in the process colonizing even those who had converted to Christianity. Christian converts were often the easiest to control and colonize. African literature from the colonial era (for example, Mongo Beti's *The Poor Christ of Bomba*[13] and Chinua Achebe's *Things Fall Apart*[14]) testifies to this. In many instances, conversion to Christianity made the process of colonization simpler. Consequently missionaries, whether knowingly or not, aided the colonial enterprise. In the eyes of many Africans, the missionaries served the colonial agents by pacifying the people – the converts – before the full force of the colonial powers forced them into submission. Mission and colonialism were viewed as two sides of the same coin – and that coin was the domination of the nations. Unfortunately, the European Christianization and colonization of Africa were basically one and the same adventure, with the latter eventually undermining the former.

To effectively colonize Africans, Indians and other Asians with a clear Christian conscience, Europeans needed to believe that they were in some way superior and that their domination of the world was God-ordained. This is how they could accept that both slavery and colonization were good for the Africans, for instance. The old theories of ethnic, cultural and religious supremacy that had been used to justify the colonization of the Americas and the enslaving of millions of Africans since the 1400s were employed once again to buttress the idea that brown and black were created to serve and to be ruled by Europeans even in Africa and Asia. Having appropriated the colonial strategies of the Europeans who had migrated to the Americas in the preceding centuries, and even the theological underpinnings of their belief in manifest destiny – that European migrants to North America were destined by God to possess the land and expand its influence in the world – many trusted that it was a God-given right for Europeans to dominate and rule the world. The colonial era saw large numbers of Europeans migrate to the colonies for economic purposes, supported by imperial power and a false ideology. They were not mere economic migrants: they were imperial colonizers, set to seize the fertile lands and to exploit local labour. The Europeans who dared to cross the seas believed that the world was theirs for the taking, and before long, tea, cotton and coffee plantations emerged in Africa, India and beyond.

By the end of the nineteenth century, then, over 20 per cent of Europe's population had migrated to the rest of the world, and this figure translates to something between 60 and 85 million Europeans (some sources suggest that not all those Europeans who migrated to Africa, Latin America and Asia are included in this figure). Sixty million is just below the population of the United Kingdom today; 85 million is slightly above the population of Germany. If we can imagine the entire population of the United Kingdom or Germany migrating to the rest of the world in one short century, that is what happened between 1814 and 1930. A majority of these Europeans were economic migrants – who happened to be Christians – taking advantage of the colonial opportunities to make a better life for themselves and their children. Only a very small percentage were actually missionaries who went with the explicit aim of evangelizing the so-called heathens and extending Christendom. However, the presence of so many European Christians in the colonies helped the missionaries tremendously. The establishing of European congregations in the colonies meant that there was a worshipping community that supported the missionaries in their work. In addition, as often happened, the missionaries used colonial powers to get their way when misunderstandings arose with the locals. The imperial powers of the colonial era really aided the cause of Christian mission. In this context of colonial mission, any talk about the blessed reflex was forgotten. Europe believed itself to be not just culturally superior, but the Christendom. It had nothing to learn from the uncivilized Africans or Asians. The black and brown peoples of Africa and Asia were to be colonized in their homelands and discouraged from migrating to Europe. Many barriers went up to prevent the colonized from contaminating Europe's hypocritical purity and accessing Europe's riches, many of which had been stolen from the colonies.

The blessed reflex is here

Today the world is quite different from what it was even 70 years ago. Key reasons for this include the collapse of the colonial empires and the subsequent emergence of post-colonial states in Africa and Asia, and then, to some people's surprise, the Christianization of many of those states, especially in Africa. We have also seen a massive shift in global migration patterns. The great European migration in which millions of Europeans relocated to the Americas first and then the rest of the world between 1500 and 1950 has slowed down significantly. In its place, multidirectional migration patterns have emerged. It is no longer just Europeans migrating to the rest of the world. Today, people are migrating in all sorts of directions. For example, Africans are migrating to Europe while Europeans are migrating to Africa. The same applies for Latin Americans and Asians. And these new migrants bring their religion with them: Africans, Asians, Latin Americans and many others are migrating to Europe along with their religion. It is because of this new migration trend that we find numerous non-Western Christians, Muslims, Sikhs, Hindus, Buddhists, and adherents of other religions from all over the world living in Western cities. Britain today is home to some of the largest Buddhist, Hindu and Sikh communities outside India and Asia. It is also home to the largest body of African Christians outside Africa. Thousands of Chinese, Korean, Filipino and Latin American Christians live in Europe today.

This is the blessed reflex. It is impossible today to talk about European Christianity without recognizing the presence of these world Christians living in Europe. Every major European city has a good number of migrant churches – Chinese, Korean, Nigerian, Ghanaian, Brazilian, and many more. The blessed reflex is here.

This presence of many non-Western Christians in the West has been made possible by two major developments. First is the rising migration trends that bring hundreds of thousands of non-Western Christians to the West every year. Second is the fact that Christianity has exploded in the majority world in the past 50 years (as it has declined in the West). The world has seen powerful spiritual revivals that have led to the conversion of millions of people in Latin America, Africa and Asia every year. At the same time, non-Western migration to the West has picked up steam. As a result, non-Western migration to the West has brought many Christians. Indeed, in some countries like the United States, migration has by design favoured Christians.

Migration

For several decades from the 1950s, regional migration around the world increased exponentially, such that by 2015 there were over 748 million internal migrants and 232 million international migrants in the world. No wonder this age that we live in has been called the 'age of migration'. Over 272 million of us today identify as international migrants, living as foreigners in countries that are not native to us for various reasons. While a majority of migrants move to countries in the same region (or continent) as their country of origin, every Westerner knows that many Africans, Asians and Latin Americans are making their way to Europe, North America, Australia and New Zealand. The current political climate in the West, however, makes some people's attitudes towards migrants rather unwelcoming. Right-wing populism has risen partly on the promise of reducing migration (by describing migrants as a threat, come to disrupt people's comfortable lives). Ever since the collapse of the European colonial project, migration has been a subject of huge contention in most Western elections. Here in the United Kingdom, the question of migration is at the heart of negotiations following the country leaving the European Union. However, plans to keep black and brown migrants from settling in Europe go back several decades, as seen in the case of the Windrush scandal.[15] In the United States, Donald Trump's rise to the presidency can partly be attributed to his very unfriendly stance on immigration. Theresa May's promise to reduce migration to a trickle while creating a hostile environment to force illegal foreigners to deport themselves was not too different from Trump's 'big and beautiful impenetrable wall' that would stop migration from Central America.

People migrate with their religions – they do not leave them behind. Whether they are Muslims or Buddhists, Christians or Jews, migrants bring their religions with them, and in many cases they embrace religion more after they arrive in their new host country. They find that religion becomes even more important in the foreign land, perhaps remaining the only steady portion of their lives amid the overwhelming sea of change they are experiencing. It also serves as an identifier, possibly separating the religious migrants from secular locals. Even if they migrate to a religious country, most migrants believe that their religious devotion, and therefore their religion, is stronger than that of the locals, as their religion back home was more fervent and purer. They attempt to hold on to that fervency and purity by forming their own migrant religious communities and allowing minimal external influence. This is a large part of the reason why migration is such a big issue in Western politics: migrants are changing the religious landscapes of Western countries. Religion makes cultural assimilation difficult.

Most non-Western migrants identify as religious and are evidently religiously active – generally more religiously active than locals. Sociologists of religion have told us for decades that as the West has been secularizing in the aftermath of World War Two, the rest of the world has become more religious. Thus, generally speaking, non-Western migrants to Europe will be more religious than Europeans. African Christians in Europe, for example, tend to be more active in their faith than the average European Christian. They often have several church activities within the week (Bible studies, prayer meetings/vigils), an evangelistic event on Saturdays, plus longer church services on Sunday. This should be expected, because for most non-Westerners, religion encompasses the whole of life. Life is impossible without religion. In the case of Africans, religion and culture are often two sides of the same coin: inseparable. The Christianization of sub-Saharan Africa in the decades after 1970 has made Africans even more religious, and as they migrate to the West they bring a religious fervour that is certainly more intense than that of the average Westerner. The process of migration itself is often a religious experience, undergirded by the prayers of their pastors, prophets and congregations back home. Religious artefacts will be among their most prized possessions: Bibles, rosaries, icons and fetishes, all carried as a symbol of God's presence. Once in the foreign land, religion makes life a little more bearable. Migrant congregations serve as safe spaces where they meet with others to process life in the diaspora.

We need to remind ourselves that when Europeans migrated around the world in the nineteenth century, they took Christianity with them. That is to say, the emergence of world Christianity is a result not just of European missionary work but also of millions of European Christians travelling to and settling in virtually all parts of the world. Today, people are migrating to the West with their religions – Christianity, Islam, Buddhism, Hinduism, Sikhism, Rastafarianism, Candomblé, and many others including African indigenous religions, and Europe has become a religious melting pot. West African Muslims are in France, Syrian Muslims are in Germany, Middle Eastern Muslims are in Britain. Nigerian Pentecostals can be found in almost every European country, though they are largely concentrated in England. Britain is also home to a great Sikh community and the largest gurdwara outside India. Hindu and Buddhist temples have mushroomed across Europe.

World Christians in Europe

Our interest is primarily on the rising presence of non-Western Christians in Europe – the blessed reflex. Two centuries ago the concept never took off, in the era of colonialism. The blessed reflex remained a footnote in mission history. But when we talk about European Christianity today, we do well to consider the many migrants that contribute to the European Christian landscape. There are currently over 10 million Africans living in Europe. Most of these come from West African countries like Nigeria, Ghana, Mali and Senegal, and North African countries including Egypt, Libya and Tunisia. However, a census of African residents in European cities would reveal people from all countries of Africa. In London – where 14 per cent of its 12 million inhabitants are of African descent, from both Africa and from the West Indies – it is quite likely that all African tribes and tongues are represented. Every major city, from Dublin to Helsinki, from Oslo to Bern, from Lisbon to Athens, has a considerable resident population of Africans. Most, especially those from sub-Saharan Africa, are Christians, and the clear evidence of their presence is the existence of African churches. Africa has many religions, but it is Pentecostal Christianity that has been the biggest export in African migration. As mentioned earlier, Africa as a continent is going through a Christian revival – with 10 million new conversions every year for the past 50 years, Christians now comprise almost 50 per cent of Africa's population, a huge rise from the 10 per cent of a hundred years ago. A simple Google search for African churches in Europe will show many Nigerian, Ghanaian, Kenyan, Zimbabwean churches in almost every major city. Many of these churches were established in the three decades between 1980 and 2010. It also happens that these 30 years are when the most African migration to Europe took place.

The presence of Africans in Europe is largely an unexpected and unintended outcome of Europe's colonization of Africa – a piece of African history that spans the years 1890 to 1970. By the time the colonies got their independence, people in the colonies had caught a glimpse of a better life in Europe. At the very least, European (or Western) education ensured access to power and influence in their countries, and many Africans began to look for ways to come to Europe to study. Governments offered scholarships to promising civil servants and youth to train at European universities. The original idea was for those who came to Europe for education to return to Africa to build their newly independent states. However, as authoritarian leadership swept across the continent, the promise of a developing Africa started to fade, and many who had come to Europe for education decided to stay (and invited their families to join them). Freedom fighters became dictators and infant democracies turned into dictatorships. The general political atmosphere of Africa became less hopeful and the economic situation became gloomier. Consequently, many more Africans migrated. In the ensuing decades, political stability has remained elusive. Today, over 50 years after independence and more than 150 *coups d'état* later, many feel there is no hope for them in the continent and are willing to risk anything to travel to Europe. The gap between the rich and the poor has continued to grow while corruption and abuse of power are rampant in government institutions. Indeed, poverty and diseases, political conflicts and civil wars, natural disasters and famines, and corruption and bad governance, among many concerns, stand in the way of many African youth wanting a better life for themselves and their children. The Mediterranean Sea continues to be a mass grave for thousands of Africans who drown as they attempt to enter Europe where they are generally not welcome.

African Christianity in Europe

African Christians exist in Europe as a result of a general migration pattern that sees thousands of Africans enter Europe every year. Just like the Europeans who left Europe in the nineteenth century, most African migrants – including asylum seekers – have come to Europe for economic reasons: to work, to study, and in search of better standards for their families. Apart from a handful of examples, we are yet to see African Christians come to Europe as missionaries. We are also yet to see African churches in Europe engage their new contexts in a missional manner. Nevertheless, the presence of African churches is growing in Europe. The Redeemed Christian Church of God (RCCG), a Pentecostal denomination from Nigeria, continues to plant more than 25 new churches each year. The Church of Pentecost (CoP), a denomination from Ghana, plants on average ten churches per year. Both these denominations planted their first congregations in Britain in the 1980s, and are growing fast in a context where Christianity is generally on the decline. The RCCG and the CoP are the two largest African denominations operating outside Africa. Other smaller networks and denominations that are growing their churches in the diaspora include the Deeper Life Church and Christ Embassy and Christ Apostolic Tabernacle. A typical African congregation in Europe will be fairly small, having 20 to 30 members, though in large cities like London African churches can have several thousand members. However, very few African churches in Europe will grow beyond 150 members. One reason for this is strategy; they tend to have many small churches instead of a few large churches, and in doing so saturate Europe with their churches. The RCCG's mission statement suggests that it seeks to 'plant churches within five minutes' walking distance in every city and town of developing countries and within five minutes' driving distance in every city and town of developed countries'.

The first African churches appeared in Europe in the 1960s; their congregations continue to exist as an exclusively African phenomenon in Europe as populations of Africans in Europe increase. Their membership is often over 90 per cent African, and they are commonly divided along national lines: Ghanaian churches, Nigerian churches, Kenyan churches, and so on. In the UK in 2015, 97 per cent of the 16,000 members of the Church of Pentecost identified as Ghanaian. The UK 2015 statistics for the Redeemed Christian Church of God are not too dissimilar; over 90 per cent of the 150,000 members were Nigerian. Very few include foreign nationals among them. Nevertheless, as Africa's Christianity grows and as Africans continue to migrate to other continents, the continent of Africa will contribute greatly to world Christianity. In some cities in Europe, Africans are slowly becoming the face of Christianity. For instance, in 2010, over 60 per cent of people who went to church on any given Sunday in London were African and Caribbean migrant Christians – most of them members of African churches or other African majority churches. Thus, people of African descent, who form only 14 per cent of London's population, make up 60 per cent of church attendance in the city. The largest congregation in Europe is the Embassy of God Church in Kiev, Ukraine, which is led by Sunday Adelaja, a Nigerian. It claims to have over 25,000 members. Its impact in Ukraine and surrounding countries has been tremendous. The second largest congregation in Europe is Matthew Ashimolowo's Kingsway International Christian Centre in London, with over 12,000 members.

Spiritual revivals and the rise of Spirit-empowered Christianities

I discussed the emergence of world Christianity earlier in Chapter 2. Let me add here something that I feel the West (or Western Christianity) needs to understand and appreciate (and yet so far seems unable to do so): the world Christianity that has emerged is decidedly spirit-oriented in nature and this is not going to change any time soon. Indeed, it seems fair to say that world Christianity *is* Pentecostalism (where Pentecostalism is used as a blanket label for all spirit-oriented Christianities). General descriptors for spirit-oriented types of Christianity include 'Pentecostal' and 'Charismatic', but what we see happening in Africa and other parts of the world is much bigger and more diverse than these Western labels can encompass. Whether we look to Africa (Nigeria, Kenya, the Democratic Republic of Congo) or Asia (South Korea), we see a type of Christianity that places great emphasis on the presence, power, gifts and workings of the Holy Spirit. It is a Christianity that recognizes the spiritual dimensions of the faith (that, as Paul calls us, we are supposed to walk in the Spirit), and also the presence of other spiritual realities that affect human life in the world.

Walter Hollenweger said that 'British Christians prayed for revival, and when it came, they did not recognize it because it was black'.[16] I would add to this statement that British Christians did not recognize the revival because it came dressed in Pentecostal clothes. Indeed, for most of us in the non-Western world, the spirit world is real and it forms the centre of understanding not just of religion but also of life in its entirety and the world as a whole. We grow up hearing talk of an invisible spirit world that is real, even more real than the material one that we can see and touch. Our cosmology includes a spirit world that is in constant interaction with the material one such that it is not possible to uphold the dichotomy between the two worlds. As an *African* Christian, I find that the theological implications of this cosmology mean that a spirit-oriented Christianity makes sense. To me this seems to be taken for granted in the New Testament even though it is never really acknowledged. As a matter of fact, in my view the cosmology of the Bible is closer to that of Africa or Asia than it is to that of Europe and the West. Jesus often spoke of spirits, demons and the devil in terms that would make sense to most non-Westerners (including those without any knowledge of Christianity). He cast out devils where we would today call for a psychotherapist, healed people where we would today refer to a surgeon. He operated in a world where many problems were resolved by dealing with the spiritual causes behind them. It is for this reason that, I believe, Pauline theology completely assumes that life in the new covenant has to be lived on a spiritual plane.

Religion serves to connect people with the spirit world. Everything else is just an add-on. People engage in religious practices in order to touch the spirit world, and a religion that does not facilitate people's connection with the spirit world ceases to be one. This was the case in Africa before the arrival of the missionaries and it continues among those Africans who have stuck with their indigenous religion. The goal of their religious practices – the songs they sing, the drums they beat and dance to, the sacrifices and libations – is basically to put them in touch with the spirit world. After converting to Christianity, these religious practices are reoriented towards the Spirit of Christ and those that are outright idolatrous are left behind. For these people in non-Christian religious contexts, the presence of the spirits has to have real-life physical implications: healings, oracles, trances. When these are lacking, they feel vulnerable – contrary spirits will overcome them. A spirit that does not extraordinarily intervene in life on their behalf is not powerful enough for them to follow; it is useless. So it is for enthusiastic Christians of the non-Western world. When the Spirit is present, it must manifest itself. It must show that it can protect people against the spiritual onslaughts of the myriad spiritual adversaries out there. This may be through gifts of healing and prophecies, inward peace, joy and hope, and other visible effects of the outworkings of the Spirit. To many in the majority world, it is non-Charismatic Christianity that is so out of the ordinary that it needs an explanation.

Pentecostalism: a very short introduction

The Pentecostal and Charismatic movements started in the early 1900s and have 750 million adherents around the world. Pentecostal and Charismatic Christians – to use the common labels – generally understand God, through the Spirit, to be accessible in the 'here and now' of life. The Spirit of God (as, of course, God is Spirit, John 4.24) acts among God's people – in their everyday ordinary lives – empowering them to carry out extraordinary acts that they could not ordinarily manage. For them, God is not distant, but is rather here with humans in their daily struggles. God can be called upon – through prayer – to intervene in their lives when needed (which is always). Of course, God must be here because there are too many evil spirits that seek to frustrate their ability to enjoy the abundant life that Christ gives. To begin to enjoy this life here and now, they must engage in spiritual warfare, and they need to pay tithes and sow seed offerings, among other things. Pentecostal Christians often engage in deep and prolonged prayer – the kind that requires night vigils and long fasts. These prayers seek to move God to act on their behalf against the many vicissitudes they face which are often put down to evil spirits that are out to trip them up or slow their progress. The prayers also increase the spiritual energy (anointing) that allows them to perform extraordinary works. But more importantly, prayers allow them to seek to hear and obey God's voice (which is usually discerned both corporately and individually).

All around the world, Pentecostal Christianity is extremely experiential. Followers like to feel the Spirit, to see the Spirit perform wonders, to hear the Spirit of God speak, and this could be through the word of prophecy or in a sermon or through many other means. They are often loud. Their worship services are generally expressive. The Spirit touches not only their spirits and bodies but also their emotions. Great services often include clapping and shouts of joy. Their prayer vigils are loud too. Many of them behave as if Jesus said that 'the kingdom of God suffers violence and the *noisy* shall take it by force' (Matt. 11.12) or as if evil spirits respond to noise. But, in their defence, noisiness is common to all spirit-centred religions, including those outside Christianity. Pentecostals are unapologetically evangelistic; often in-your-face kind of evangelistic. They believe they must save as many people as possible from the 'eternal damnation of hell fire'. This is needed especially in our day and age which they believe is the last of the last days (Acts 2.17, also Joel 2.28, and note that Peter changes Joel's 'afterwards' to 'in the last days'). To achieve this, they must attempt to convert everyone on their way, even those they deem to be in dead denominations. We see them giving out Christian tracts on the high streets of Britain. They generally want to convert people not just to Pentecostalism but to their type of Pentecostalism (which is usually problematic).

In addition, we must note that most non-Western Pentecostals are biblicist in their reading of the Bible. They love the Bible and take it to be true to the letter; they believe what has been written in the Word without any filters. If the Bible says, 'you are healed', it shows lack of faith to say or believe otherwise. The Bible says Christ became poor so we may be rich, and this they often believe literally, standing upon God's Word. Whose report do you believe? Do you believe the doctor or the Bible? Often this leads to an otherworldly faith that does not know how to respond eloquently to life struggles. What happens when sickness is not healed? Or when the expected riches do not arrive? I have seen Pentecostal pastors literally stand upon a Bible while praying to show that they are standing on God's Word, fully believing that whatever it says will come to pass. My favourite childhood memory is of hearing our elders remind God of what God says in the Bible so that God can bring them to fruition: 'You said in your word that those who trust in you will not be put to shame; remove this shame from us'. While Pentecostals love the Bible and know it well, they can be suspicious of theology and theological education, especially Western theology. The Pentecostal movement is highly biblically literate and yet often theologically disinterested. Many still believe that all the minister needs is the Spirit. The anointing is the primary tool for every minister. Everything else, including a good theological understanding of the Bible and ministry, is secondary.

Pentecostalism is a mobile Christianity. It has exploded in the parts of the world where people are extremely mobile – moving from rural to urban areas, from one part of the country to another, from one country to another in the same region, and from one continent to another. This is the case in Latin America, Africa and parts of Asia. Many Pentecostals see the Spirit's work in their migration. They seek God's help in their migration. The Spirit, like the wind, is always moving, and so should they be. Jesus' words to the disciples 'to go into all the nations' imply movement and migration. As they migrate from one place to another, they are moving with the Spirit in obedience to Christ, even if their migration is for non-religious reasons. The Spirit empowers them to evangelize wherever they are, at home or overseas. The Spirit makes them all evangelists (and missionaries). Pentecostal faith also often enables members to have social mobility. As it spreads among non-Western peoples in Latin America, Africa and Asia, Pentecostalism has gained great acceptance among poor people. It often preaches economic empowerment. Some pastors teach their members financial management and a good work ethic. Other churches go further, providing vocational training or scholarships in all stages of education. Others will run social enterprises like schools and hospitals where their members can gain employment. Generally speaking, the Pentecostal message encourages people to be responsible with their finances. Money that might have been spent on beer or mistresses now becomes available to the family, improving their quality of life and thus making them upwardly mobile. Most Pentecostals encourage members to bring their 'tithes to the storehouse' so that the church is empowered to help the needy in society. Those who do not tithe are said to be robbing God (Mal. 3.10). Then there is the controversial prosperity gospel that takes the promise of God's provision and turns it into a money-making ploy that some ministers use to sell spiritual power and blessings.

Pentecostal denominational polity is diverse. Each Pentecostal church will be different from the others around it. They have no universal lectionary. Their liturgy is always fluid, depending on contextual factors and usually flowing *as the Spirit leads*. Many of them have an open ecclesiology that is said to be shaped around the 'leading of the Spirit' – a phrase that is a ready excuse for bad planning, poor preparation and a perpetual inability to keep to a schedule. Most Pentecostal churches are independent, isolated and autonomous. The pastor and the board make all the decisions. If they belong to a family of churches, it will be either an association of loosely affiliated independent churches (in which case, all decisions are made locally within the congregation) or a denominational structure headquartered somewhere in the Global South (where all major decisions are made and must be consulted in almost everything). Independent Pentecostal pastors will often have a relationship with a bishop or an apostle for spiritual covering – a semi-formal arrangement that seeks to provide access to larger networks of Pentecostal pastors and sometimes a praying community.

Walter Hollenweger's indictment about not recognizing revival because it was black could apply equally to it coming dressed in Pentecostal garb. It is not just different in complexion, it is different in its cultural self-expression. It is also different in its theology. The revival has come looking radically different from both the British Christianity that sent missionaries to Africa 200 years ago and the British Christianity that is here now. It does not look like a typical Church of England Christianity. A great deal of what British Christians know about Pentecostalism comes through mainstream media and focuses on the troublesome aspects of Pentecostalism, such as poor contextualization, prosperity gospel, loud vigils, flamboyant pastors. However, there is a lot more to the movement than the often misinformed images in the tabloids. Pentecostals are here to stay. It is impossible to imagine a world Christianity in which Pentecostalism is absent. Generations of world Christians have never belonged to a non-Pentecostal church. Going forward, it will be helpful for Europeans to accept and understand Pentecostals as fellow members of the body of Christ present here in Europe today. Good leaders will take time to learn of Pentecostalism.

Browsing through any directory of black majority churches in Britain will make it evident that African Christianity in Britain is Pentecostal in its outlook and expression. It is no different in Europe. As mentioned earlier, outstanding African denominations in Europe include the likes of the Redeemed Christian Church of God and the Church of Pentecost along with many smaller networks of African churches in Europe. From West Africa, we have the Christ Apostolic Church and its sister denominations, the Apostolic Church of Nigeria and the Apostolic Church of Ghana. The Apostolic Faith Mission is a South African denomination that has congregations scattered around European cities. All these denominations identify themselves as Pentecostal in their faith tradition. However, even those African Christians who do not attend these Pentecostal churches will most likely have been somewhat influenced by the Pentecostal outlook or, to say the least, Charismatic Christianity. Zimbabwean Anglicans, Malawian Presbyterians and Ghanaian Methodists, just like many other African Christians in Europe, will tend to be sympathetic to and show Charismatic tendencies in their fellowships. For African Pentecostals, the label itself is of increasingly significant importance in Europe as they believe that it distinguishes them from the largely nominal form of Christianity they see in European churches – and thus justifies their sense of call to evangelize Europe. Being a Pentecostal testifies of their *personal* commitment to the Lord and their passion for his work in the world – a commitment evidenced by their public relationship with the Spirit. It clearly sets them apart from mainstream Christians who are usually characterized as spiritually lacking and their churches lifeless and boring.

The growth of African Christianity in Europe is reason enough for optimism. There is a hopeful future for Christianity in a continent that has seen dwindling numbers of Christians for decades. God is bringing to Europe Christians from other parts of the world to renew and reinvigorate European Christianity. Politically, they may be seen as economic migrants but in God's grand scheme of mission they are the ambassadors, the salt and light that Christ has in Europe in this day and age. Of course, by their sheer numbers, foreign Christians make an impact on the religious landscape of Europe in a significant way – Africans have reversed the church decline in London! Many of the largest congregations in Europe are African. The fastest growing church-planting movements are African. British Christians prayed for revival, but when it came they could not recognize it because it was black and Pentecostal.

Nevertheless, we need to be cautious in our optimism. African Christian presence in Europe has not yet resulted in the evangelization of Europeans. African churches are often true to their name right across Europe; they are African churches in both culture and membership, with a negligibly small number of Europeans in their midst. Even the large African denominations in Europe who have enough financial resources to invest in cross-cultural ministry have struggled to connect with Europeans. The main reason for this, in my view, is that African churches in Europe usually self-identify, rather proudly, as Pentecostal or Charismatic, when Europeans, generally speaking, are wary of Pentecostalism. In Britain, I have come to learn that the 'excesses' of Pentecostalism go against the values of a culture that loves moderation.[17] To most Europeans, Pentecostalism is grounded in the 'health and wealth' gospel – a gospel that many European Christians deride. African Pentecostal pastors leading megachurches in Britain are often covered negatively in the media for their flamboyant lifestyles and their preaching of the prosperity gospel. In addition, African Pentecostals tend to put a great deal of emphasis on the power and work of the Holy

Spirit, which makes sense in a spirit-centred worldview of the Africans. Europeans, however, live in a secular post-Enlightenment worldview where spirits (and God) are too far away to be of any relevance to human life. In the language of Charles Taylor, Westerners (including Europeans) live as buffered selves in a world devoid of spirits.[18] The Pentecostal focus on the Spirit and the spirit world – the belief in a Holy Spirit that acts as God in human life in real and tangible ways – is antithetical to the beliefs of many British and European Christians. (For them, the Spirit is a doctrine, a part of the transcendent and far-distant triune God that only causes chaos when it comes into contact with human beings.) This essentially means that the Africans' Pentecostal identity often hinders their witness to Europeans.

While the spirit-empowered Pentecostal Christianity makes a critique of the Enlightenment-shaped European Christianity – that Christianity is powerless without the Spirit – it must contextualize itself and rethink the way it tries to share the gospel with a people for whom pneumatic Christianity is a stumbling block. As we have seen, Pentecostal and Charismatic Christianity has spread like wildfire while non-Charismatic and non-Pentecostal Christianities have declined massively, both in number and in influence. The Africans in Europe find confidence in the fact that their Pentecostal churches are more energetic and growing while those of their British counterparts are losing members. They want to remind Europeans that the Christianity that their missionaries brought to Africa has not been able to sustain itself in Europe – and that the Africans received it and have transformed it into something new that has actually grown exponentially. It is this new type of Christianity that the Africans bring that may eventually be able to challenge European secularism. For now, however, the very thing that makes African Christianity strong is what makes it largely unattractive to Europeans – its Pentecostal or Charismatic identity. It is especially unhelpful that their efforts at evangelizing Europeans seem to seek to convert them not just to Christianity but also to an African form of Pentecostalism. This, I believe, is an impossible task.

Even though many of these non-Western churches are patronized almost exclusively by non-Westerners and are unable to evangelize beyond their own fellow nationals, there is evidence that their presence is actually invigorating British Christianity. For instance, when we talk about Christianity in London today, we have to consider African and Caribbean Christians, both in Pentecostal churches and in mainstream churches, because the presence of these non-Western Christians and their churches means that Christianity is in fact on the rise and churches are growing again in London. Consequently, while we acknowledge that non-Western missionary work among Westerners is yet to blossom, we must celebrate that non-Western Christians are strengthening the presence of Christianity in some cities, including through their prayers and ministries of mercy. Their presence in Britain brings with it gifts that in many ways invigorate both British culture and British Christianity. It is the argument of this book that a proper engagement between British and non-Western Christians resident in Britain will enrich British Christianity, and hopefully help it rediscover its missional impulses to re-evangelize Britain.

African churches fail to make good connections with European churches – the churches that would help them begin to understand European culture and explore what they need to do in order to contextualize their ministries for mission among Europeans. On the one hand, we have Africans who have a zeal for evangelism, engaging in street or door-knocking evangelism, using strategies that worked in Africa but yield minimal results in Britain. On the other hand, we have British Christians who often cannot talk about their faith in public, let alone engage in evangelism, and yet they know about British culture. If these two groups could work together, we could possibly see a missionary movement that would effectively engage in evangelism in Britain.

Notes

1 David B. Barrett et al., *World Christian Trends, AD 30–AD 2200: Interpreting the Annual Christian Megacensus* (Pasadena, CA: William Carey Library, 2001).

2 Coptic Christianity has existed in Egypt right from the first century of Christianity when Mark the Evangelist established the See of Alexandria. Ethiopian Christianity goes back to the fourth century CE.

3 Commission on World Mission and Evangelism and Ronald Kenneth Orchard, *Witness in Six Continents: Records of the Meeting of the Commission on World Mission and Evangelism of the World Council of Churches held in Mexico City, December 8th to 19th, 1963* (London: Edinburgh House Press, 1964), p. 1.

4 Michael W. Goheen, *Introducing Christian Mission Today: Scripture, History, and Issues* (Downers Grove, IL: IVP Academic, 2014), p. 25.

5 Norimitsu Onishi, 'Korean Missionaries Carrying Word to Hard-to-Sway Places', *The New York Times* (New York) 2004, www.nytimes.com/2004/11/01/world/asia/korean-missionaries-carrying-word-to-hardtosway-places.html?_r=0 (accessed 12.10.19).

6 Onishi, 'Korean Missionaries'.

7 Harvey Kwiyani, *Sent Forth: African Missionary Work in the West*, American Society of Missiology Series (Maryknoll, NY: Orbis, 2014), p. 59.

8 For more on this subject, see Mark Sturge, *Look What the Lord has Done!*

An Exploration of Black Christian Faith in Britain (Bletchley: Scripture Union, 2005).

9 *Changing Faiths: Latinos and the Transformation of American Religion*, The Pew Research Center, 2007.

10 Virgilio P. Elizondo, *The Future is Mestizo: Life Where Cultures Meet*, Meyer-Stone (ed.) (Oak Park, IL: Meyer-Stone Books, 1988).

11 Gastón Espinosa, *Latino Pentecostals in America: Faith and Politics in Action* (Cambridge, MA: Harvard University Press, 2014). Also see New Life Covenant Church, 'Our Church: Our Leadership', 2019, www.mynewlife.org/our-church-extended (accessed 15.10.19).

12 Henry M. Stanley, *Through the Dark Continent: Or, The Sources of the Nile Around the Great Lakes of Equatorial Africa, and Down the Livingstone River to the Atlantic Ocean*, 2 vols (New York: Harper, 1878); Joseph Conrad, Fiona Banner and Paolo Pellegrin, *Heart of Darkness* (London: Four Corners Books, 2015).

13 Mongo Beti, *The Poor Christ of Bomba* (Long Grove, IL: Waveland, 1971).

14 Chinua Achebe, *Things Fall Apart* (New York: McDowell, 1959).

15 David Olusoga's work on the history of the Windrush scandal is revealing. See his *Black and British: A Forgotten History* (London: Macmillan, 2016).

16 Roswith Gerloff, 'Foreword' in *A Plea for British Black Theologies: The Black Church Movement in Britain in its Transatlantic Cultural and Theological Interaction with Special References to the Pentecostal Oneness (Apostolic) and Sabbatarian Movements*, Studien zur Interkulturellen Geschichte des Christentums (Frankfurt am Main: P. Lang, 1992).

17 By excesses of Pentecostalism, they meant such things as night vigils and distribution of gospel tracts on the streets.

18 Charles Taylor, *A Secular Age* (Cambridge, MA: Belknap Press of Harvard University Press, 2007), pp. 37–9.

5

The Multicultural Kingdom is Here

The world is changing, and in many aspects much faster than we seem to recognize, and involving changes that are not easily reversible. On a global scale, I believe we are living in a period of great transition. We are seeing an old world order struggling to stay relevant as a new order seems inevitable. Barely a hundred years ago, European domination of the world was taken for granted. The British empire, commonly described as 'the empire upon which the sun never sets', spanned right across the globe, from Vancouver to Nyasaland and Burma to Hong Kong. The Spanish empire at its peak 200 years earlier also claimed to be an empire upon which the sun never set. We have seen the rise of the American empire, which through the USA's military presence desires to spread democracy around the world. But as the American empire begins to crack at the seams, a new world order is emerging – one in which Britain is retreating from the European Union and the United States is arguing over a wall that some Americans believe will reduce migration from Latin America. It is a fair estimation that post-Brexit Britain will be totally different from the Britain that had many colonies spread around the world only 70 years ago. As the West struggles to hold itself together, we are seeing Russia, China and India assert themselves as key players in global geopolitics.

At the centre of the perceived chaos of this new world is the subject of migration. Historically, empires sent their people to migrate to their colonies. The Greeks sent their people as far as Persia. The Romans had their people living as far away as Britain and Morocco. The Portuguese migrated as far as India; the Spanish empire had numerous citizens migrate to Latin America in the sixteenth and seventeenth centuries. Millions of Europeans migrated from Europe to the rest of the world in the nineteenth century alone. Around 20 per cent of Europe's population migrated to other parts of the world in the years between 1814 and 1930 – and this amounted to more than 60 million Europeans.[1] In these days of an American empire, many thousands of American citizens are living – or are stationed – all over the world: in Germany, Djibouti, the Philippines. This has been described as globalization from above, but in a world of great uncertainty we are also witnessing globalization from below – the migration of people from the rest of the world to the West. There is always a high level of anxiety in the West around the subject of migration, and this is because, generally speaking, current migration trends bring people from the rest of the world to the West, and many Westerners believe the immigrants are only coming to use up their resources. Both the marginalized and the colonized – or the formerly colonized – are now seeking to assert themselves in ways that were not possible a century ago. The world is constantly changing, and so should the Church.

The myth of a monocultural Britain

To demographic historians of Britain, it is obvious that this island has, for the larger part of two millennia, always been a society of many cultures, a diverse and heterogeneous society. David Olusoga, for example, has spoken about the presence of Africans in Britain long before the transatlantic slave trade. Many other ethnic groups have been present in Britain for centuries too. People who considered themselves indigenous British today have descended from various groups who have settled in Britain over many centuries. Different ethnic tribes settled in various parts of Britain, and as they came and went they all left their own legacies, many of which still exist today. The Celts lived in Britain from the first millennium BCE, but before them a group of various ethnicities labelled together as 'Pre-Celts' are said to have been here from the time of the last ice age. The Celts were pushed into Scotland, Wales and Cornwall after the Roman invasion of 43 CE following which the Romans settled in Britain, and ruled England until the fall of the empire. Because of the size of the empire and the need to move people, especially the army from one side of the empire to the other, the Romans brought with them to Britain people from as far as Africa and Persia. We learn of Africans living in Britain in the Roman era. It may seem to be a joke that Africans patrolled Hadrian's Wall in the north of England, but it is historical fact that Africans did indeed live in Yorkshire during Roman times. Following the collapse of Roman influence and authority there came the Angles, Saxons, Danes, Vikings and Normans. Jewish settlers started to arrive after 1066, brought by William the Conqueror. The Roma started to arrive in the sixteenth century. The oldest black British community in Britain lived in Liverpool from the 1730s as Liverpool was involved in the transatlantic slave trade. The Chinese community in Britain dates back to the arrival of Chinese seamen in the nineteenth century. Over the centuries, thousands of people have arrived in Britain as refugees from countries such as France, Ireland and Russia, escaping persecution or famine. In addition, let us not forget those twentieth-century immigrants who have arrived since the end of the war and the fall of the European colonial empires: Afro-Caribbean, Indian, Pakistani, Bangladeshi, more Chinese. To these are added Europeans, from Germany, Italy and Portugal to the Scandinavian countries, together with Poles and Russians, Australasians, Arabs, Nigerians, Ghanaians, South Africans, Moroccans, Somalians, South and North Americans.

Multicultural Britain

The story of Britain's multiculturalism is unique in many ways. At its peak, Britain had the largest empire in history, and it thus had to deal with many cultures around the world. In 1920 the British empire covered 24 per cent of the earth's land surface, and more than 23 per cent of the world's population (which was more than 400 million people). At the end of the nineteenth century, Queen Victoria had more Muslim subjects than any Muslim ruler in the world. The British Raj (starting as early as 1858) put the Queen in charge of millions of Hindus and Buddhists. When India and Pakistan became independent in 1947, millions of their citizens would continue to be citizens of the British Commonwealth – which came with rights, at least on paper, similar to British citizens who were born in Britain itself. It was also during the era of the empire that the British government faced many expressions of African religion, and in response thousands of missionaries were encouraged to go to the colonies to convert Africans from their own religions to Christianity.

The 2011 census showed that 14 per cent of the population living in the UK were from a minority ethnic group. This is a significant increase from 2001 when only 7 per cent identified as ethnic minorities. It makes sense to anticipate that by 2021 the percentage of ethnic minorities will have increased further. People from all cultures and ethnicities can be found in every corner of Britain and each person contributes to make Britain the place it is today. If you walk down a street in Britain, especially in the bigger cities, many of the people you will see will be British people, but they all look different because the people of Britain are a mixed race.

In 2017, about 86 per cent of the UK population were UK-born and about 90 per cent were British nationals – down from about 89 per cent and 93 per cent respectively in 2007. Thus 14 per cent of UK residents were born outside the UK while 7 per cent are citizens of other countries. The population census of 2011 highlighted that in England and Wales 80 per cent of the population were white British. Asian (Pakistani, Indian, Bangladeshi, other) 'groups' made up 6.8 per cent of the population;

black groups 3.4 per cent, Chinese groups 0.7 per cent, Arab groups 0.4 per cent, and other groups 0.6 per cent. In 2011, 45 per cent (3.7 million) of London's 8.2 million residents were white British. The census also showed that 87 per cent of the population of England and Wales were born in the UK. Of those not born in the UK, 9 per cent were born in India, 8 per cent in Poland and 6 per cent in Pakistan. It also revealed that African migrants surpassed Caribbeans in the UK in the ten years between 2001 and 2011.

London is now the most diverse city in the world, with more than 300 languages spoken in it. More than 50 non-indigenous communities are said to have populations of 10,000 or more in London. It is likely that every race, culture and religion in the world – or, in the biblical language, every nation, tribe and tongue – can claim at least a handful of Londoners. The 2011 census showed that only 45 per cent of the 8.1 million Londoners identify as white British, while 5 per cent considered themselves to be of mixed race. Phil Wood and Charles Landry comment:

> London's Muslim population of 607,083 people is probably the most diverse anywhere in the world, besides Mecca ... The rest of Britain is now changing ... There are 37,000 Pakistan-born people in Birmingham and 27,500 in Bradford, 25,000 Indians in Leicester, 4,000 Bangladeshis in Oldham and 4,000 West Indians in Nottingham. There are now over 1,000 French people living in Bristol and Brighton, 650 Greeks in Colchester, 600 Portuguese in Bournemouth and Poole, 800 Poles in Bradford, 1,300 Somalis in Sheffield, 770 Zimbabweans in Luton, 370 Iranians in Newcastle and 400 in Stockport, and 240 Malaysians in Southsea. And these figures represent only those who are foreign born and not the much larger numbers of second-generation and beyond people whose nationality and identity will be hyphenated.[2]

Cultural diversity is on the rise everywhere, and here in Britain one of the most prevalent indicators is ethnic diversity. The work of such research centres as the University of Manchester's Centre on Dynamics of Ethnicity (UM-CoDE) is helpful, and in 2012 they published a report entitled, *How Has Ethnic Diversity Grown 1991–2002–2011?* Their research concluded that:

> In 2011, the ethnic group population other than White British accounted for 20% (or 11 million) of the population of England and Wales compared with 14% (or 7 million) in 2001 ... Despite this growth, the White British ethnic group represents the majority (80%) of the population. The total ethnic group population other than White has more

than doubled in size since 1991, from 3 million (or 7%) to almost 8 million (or 14%). The White population remained static in total size between 1991 and 2001, and increased marginally between 2001 and 2011. The White British population, measured separately for the first time in 2001, declined by 1% between 2001 and 2011, whereas the White Irish population decreased by 18%.[3]

Cultural diversity is always a difficult subject to discuss. Quite often, it attracts value judgements in response – is cultural diversity good or bad? Is any type of diversity good at all? Should we encourage diversity in our schools, churches, or society as a whole? Whether we say it is good or bad, it is quickly connected to migration, as it is generally through migration that cultural diversity occurs. So, there is usually an underlying question about migration. Is migration good for us and our country? Are migrants good to have among us? The answer varies depending on who is talking. Many will say that cultural diversity is good, as are other forms of diversity, for example ethnicity or class. It can be argued that diversity makes possible crossbreeding of ideas, and in so doing helps societies progress. Without this exchange of ideas between insiders and outsiders, societies stagnate for lack of fresh thinking. One of the most convincing arguments is made by Richard Pascale, Mark Millemann and Linda Gioja in *Surfing the Edge of Chaos*.[4] The 'law of requisite variety', according to the authors, states that, 'the survival of any system depends on its capacity to cultivate – and not just tolerate – variety in its internal structure'. They add that prolonged equilibrium dulls a society's senses and saps its ability to arouse itself appropriately in the face of danger.[5] In a nutshell, every society needs variety if it is to survive. In the conversation of cultural diversity, this law of requisite variety suggests something that my Lhomwe peoples of Malawi know well: 'oftentimes, it takes a stranger to move the society forward'.

Others propose strong arguments against cultural diversity, a prominent one being the idea that entertaining any form of cultural diversity means a loss of cultural purity. This line of thought can be heard in contemporary political circles. 'If we allow people of a different culture to live among us *without forcing them to conform to our culture*,' the argument goes, 'they will make us lose our culture.' They fail to realize that culture is always shaped by external factors as much as it is by internal ones. This whole idea of a cultural purity in any society is an illusion. This is why political multiculturalism has been said to be a failure. For several decades now, secular conversations about multiculturalism in the West have emphasized the need for assimilation.[6] Overall, this has not been successful, and multiculturalism is now thought to be a failed project in

Europe, where one political leader after another in the past five years has condemned the idea as unworkable.[7]

The message from studies of migration by experts in the field is loud and clear; we live in the 'age of migration'.[8] The UN migration data estimate that in 2019 there were over 272 million migrants in the world, defining 'migrant' to be any person who changes his or her usual country of residence.[9] This represents 3.4 per cent of the world's total population. When compared to 173 million migrants in 2000 (2.8 per cent) and 102 million migrants in 1980 (2.3 per cent), this shows a steady rise in migrant populations in the world. The recent House of Commons' Migration Statistics Briefing Paper (published 22 October 2019) indicates that there are 6.1 million people living in the UK who have the nationality of a different country (down from 6.2 million in 2018). This reflects 9 per cent of the total population. There are 3.6 million EU nationals (excluding UK, down from 3.7 million in 2018) living in the UK while 785,000 UK nationals live in other EU countries excluding Ireland.

Minority-dominated neighbourhoods are becoming more common by the year, suggesting high concentrations of immigrants in areas of some cities in the West. In the United States, sociologists and demographers believe that by 2050 there will be no majority-minority racial distinctions. The UK may be slower to move in that direction, but cultural diversity is increasing. Part of the reason is the low birth rate among white Europeans, while that of minorities, especially Hispanics, is quite high. The population of the United States will thus keep increasing, but mainly from non-Caucasian Americans because of both the birthrate and immigration.

Cultural diversity: how do we respond?

The subject of multicultural Christianity is new to most of us. Our theologies, missiologies and ecclesiologies are yet to catch up with the reality of the culturally diverse world we see in our Western cities. Religion and race are two concepts yet to be fully negotiated within Christianity. Race relations within the Christian community is a contentious issue, and will become more so as the distance between Christians in different parts of the world diminishes, and globalization intensifies as this century progresses. As we stand today, the subject of racial segregation in Christianity must be explored. In most of Western Christianity, to talk about race is to open the scars of the racism of the past – something we do not need to talk about since Christianity is working just fine as it is right now. In the United States, Christian churches are very segregated communities, with over 92 per cent of congregations being mono-ethnic.[10] Here in Britain, there is no conclusive data, but scholars such as Israel Olofinjana put the figures at 60 to 65 per cent of all congregations being monocultural.

The cultural diversity we see within Christianity in Britain is the direct result of two main factors – the exploding of Christianity in Latin America, Africa and parts of Asia, and changing migration patterns – both of which gained a great deal of momentum in the second half of the twentieth century, and particularly in the last quarter. This cultural diversity is not a passing phenomenon, and as we go deeper into the twenty-first century, the world will become more and more multicoloured. Seismic shifts are already taking place, changing the cultural and ethnic compositions in many cities and towns.

Rejection and welcome

Living in Western Europe and North America in the early decades of the twenty-first century feels quite paradoxical. Migrants can never be sure whether they are welcome or not, and, contrary to the nice words of politicians and men of God, many migrants feel rejected and unwelcome. We are currently seeing the resurgence of nationalism (even among Christians); it is beginning to reshape a great deal of Western politics. Donald Trump, enabled largely by his evangelical base, is still trying to build a wall to prevent (black and brown) migrants from entering the country from Central America. In Europe, Britain is retreating from the EU, back to being just the small island nation it once was before it ruled 25 per cent of the world. Christians in Europe and North America, and especially in Britain, tend to be ambivalent about the subject of migration. Some argue that the strangers among us deserve at least to be made welcome. Others believe that only those who are in the West legally should expect to be welcomed – which of course means that those who are not here legally are not welcome. Then there is the anti-migration sentiment that even those who are in the West legally are using up resources that belong to the 'owners of the land'. Such a narrative usually states that migrants come to Britain to take jobs that belong to Western people or live on benefits. Christian leaders fail to make an informed and united response to this. As a result, migrants (including Christian migrants) tend to live with the ambiguities of belonging while not fully belonging at the same time.

Generally speaking, migration is a contested issue in Western politics and the lengths to which Westerners go to prevent migrants from reaching Europe and North America mean that it makes sense that migrants often feel unwelcome and unwanted. The challenge for Western Christians is that it is really difficult to share Holy Communion with people whose presence among us is a problem. Whether we are talking about barricading the English Channel or building a wall on the Texas–Mexico border, or trying to make sense of the plight of the Windrush generation who are being deported back to Jamaica after 50 years of living in Britain, we are, as followers of Christ, confronted by the fact that Christ would side with the migrants – that the Scriptures are sympathetic to the stranger and the foreigner among us. It has been argued eloquently that Christ himself was an immigrant – that our God is an immigrant God. But does the Bible require Christians to be hospitable even when their governments are becoming hostile?

Societies respond to cultural diversity in many and varied ways, from racist anti-immigration white supremacist Trump supporters shouting 'build that wall' to super-biblicist Christians who take the Bible in its most literal sense and minister hospitality to undocumented immigrants, to colour-blind post-racial intellectuals who are indifferent about the colour of anything in life. In general, the Western Church's response to the migration of foreign Christians and the cultural diversity that emerges out of their presence in the West has been ambivalent, if not contradictory. Migrant Christians, just like any other migrants, threaten to become Europeans and therefore have access to and possibly exploit the commonwealth entitled to Europeans. The issues of land, wealth and national identity are always difficult to negotiate. At a denominational gathering discussing how to respond to the Syrian refugee crisis in London in 2016, I was touched to hear one British pastor (with a German name) wonder how the Canaanites felt knowing that their land was Israel's promised land. 'How should I – as a British person – feel about migration when I know that these British islands that I call home are somebody else's promised land?' His concerns made sense; the only problem we had was the fact that his own grandfather was an immigrant too, and he still had relatives in Germany. His bishop responded by reminding him that 'the whole world is the Lord's; it is God's right to mix the nations every so often. God is the host; we are all foreigners at God's table.'

Christians are divided in their response to the issue of migration. One theological position argues that verses like Leviticus 19.34 – 'The alien who resides with you shall be to you as the citizen among you; you shall love the alien as yourself, for you were aliens in the land of Egypt: I am the Lord your God' – require us to be hospitable to strangers no matter what, and that no human being can be (an) illegal (immigrant). Others have argued that the laws of the sovereign nation state must be obeyed no matter what, and that they supersede the laws of the Old Testament. A commonly used Scripture to support this is Romans 13.1–3:

> Let every person be subject to the governing authorities; for there is no
> authority except from God, and those authorities that exist have been
> instituted by God. Therefore whoever resists authority resists what God
> has appointed, and those who resist will incur judgement. For rulers are
> not a terror to good conduct, but to bad. Do you wish to have no fear of
> the authority? Then do what is good, and you will receive its approval.

It is within the power of the government, then – and rightly so – to control
migration. Christians are therefore required to obey whatever laws the
government establishes. Thus, if the government does not recognize a
person as a legal or documented migrant, Christians ought to refuse to
have anything to do with them.

There are several ways of dealing with the cultural diversity that ensues
where migrants have settled in a city or a church. The following three
ways are the most common.

1 Assimilation

Assimilation is the most popular. Assimilation assumes that new migrants
will be thrown into the mainstream of the dominant culture, where they
have to assimilate – to let go of their cultures and to embrace the culture
of their new host society – in order to belong. People are required to
integrate into the predominant values of the culture of their new home,
and leave their home cultures aside. The immigrants are expected to
change to fit into the new amalgam of values that make the dominant
culture. Countries like the United States understand assimilation using the
metaphor of a melting pot – whatever you add into the pot adds to and
takes on the flavour of the contents, gradually losing its distinctiveness –
it becomes less strong and ultimately disappears. Immigrants often need
to forget everything of their old culture in order to assimilate successfully,
for instance having to learn the language as soon as possible (and not for-
getting to get the accent right – this is what makes you American). Thus
migrants are always under pressure to adapt to the existing way of life as
quickly as possible for the sake of their survival.

2 Cultural pluralism

Assimilation does not work so well in the face of the rapid cultural
changes that shape life in Western cities. Cultures are never static long
enough for the new people to figure out how best to adapt. In addition,

it is not straightforward to demand that people let go of their identity to become something they are not; assimilation always creates groups of marginalized and isolated people who end up feeling unwelcome. Cultural pluralism emerges as an option, in which the core values and customs of the dominant culture are to be acquired, but ethnic minorities are allowed to preserve their home values and customs, provided these do not interfere with those of the dominant society. Cultural pluralism is more politically correct than assimilation, even though it still maintains the language of 'this is the way we do it here'. The dominant culture determines what is allowable on the public domain. In countries like Australia, immigrants are expected to publicly declare that all things of the dominant culture are best.

3 Multiculturalism

Assimilation and pluralism have been criticized for not taking other cultures seriously; in both, the culture of the host society decides what is acceptable in the public arena and what is not. In their place, many now prefer multiculturalism – a recent phenomenon where dominant and minority cultures interact respectfully and enrich each other. Multiculturalism is essentially a commitment by all to the existence of different cultural groups as sanctioned entities that maintain some separate structures but with some structures held in common by all groups in society. The dignity of all the cultures is maintained while together they shape the common culture. In other words, there is no dominant culture.

Against the metaphor of a melting pot, multiculturalism creates a mosaic where many individual pieces of different colours combine to make a colourful, pleasing whole. Another popular metaphor is that of a salad bowl in which all ingredients work together without losing their unique flavour. It holds that some differences between individuals and groups are potential sources of beauty, strength and renewal, rather than of misunderstandings and strife. It values the diverse perspectives people develop and maintain through varieties of experiences and backgrounds stemming from racial, ethnic, gender, sexual orientation and/or class differences in our society. It strives to uphold the ideals of equality, equity and freedom, and encourages respect for individuals and groups as a principle that is fundamental to the societal success.

Welcoming the stranger

One of these three models of responding to migration and cultural diversity, or some combination of them, needs to work, otherwise we remain with exclusion and isolation, which is detrimental to both the migrants and the host nations. It is the hope of this book that we will find a way for global Christians in Britain to worship together while celebrating diversity – to make Christian multiculturalism work. My thoughts on this are shaped significantly by Charles Taylor, who eloquently argues in his essay on multiculturalism entitled 'The Politics of Recognition' that we need to be able to recognize the unique identity of any individual or group, their distinctiveness from everyone else.[11] For Taylor, assimilation is the cardinal sin against the ideal of authenticity.[12] Against those who argue for blindness to difference, Taylor suggests that recognizing particularity allows individuals to strengthen their identity, and therefore their authenticity.[13] In essence, he is calling for the politics of equal recognition – a move from honour to dignity – emphasizing the equal dignity of all citizens, which in turn entails the equalization of rights and entitlements. Everyone deserves to be recognized, even migrants. Using theories from Immanuel Kant and Jean-Jacques Rousseau, Taylor suggests that 'a multicultural society with strong collective goals can be liberal provided it is capable of respecting diversity, especially when dealing with those who do not share its common goals'.[14] The politics of equal respect that is inhospitable to difference is problematic, because it insists on uniform application of the rules defining these rights without exception, and it is suspicious of collective goals. He draws from Hans-Georg Gadamer's theory of the 'fusion of horizons' to argue that multiculturalism enables us to move on to a broader horizon, where it is possible to live respectfully with each other without overpowering one another.[15]

Another voice that speaks to us in Britain is that of Gerald Arbuckle. In his book *Earthing the Gospel* Arbuckle suggests that multiculturalism is grounded upon several assumptions.[16] The first is that the meeting of different cultures can bring a richness of values to all, including the host culture. The stress is on fostering the spirit of positive acceptance or recognition of cultural difference. Second is a duality of interaction: positive adjustment is necessary on the part of both immigrant and host culture, through a process of positive and dynamic interaction or intercultural mutuality. Third, only from a position of cultural strength will migrants be able to move out to contact other cultures with a sense of identity, self-respect and confidence. Each of these assumptions applies in Britain. Good hospitality empowers the stranger to participate as an equal. The blessing of cultural diversity that we see in British cities today calls for a multicultural approach to church and mission. We must remember that the origin of black churches in Britain is tied to the experiences of the Windrush generation of migrants from the West Indies. When they arrived in Britain and went to British churches, they felt unwelcome, and as a result they formed their own congregations. Later African migrants also felt unwelcome in British churches, and they followed the pattern set by the Afro-Caribbeans, and formed African churches.

I am also convinced that the multicultural context of (urban) Britain needs a multicultural missionary movement. African, Latin American, Asian and British Christians need to work together in mission. For that to happen, there needs to be some intentional collaboration. Congregational leaders may need to model this for their followers by working together more visibly. I anticipate that the body of Christ in Britain can model racial reconciliation for the world by living an alternative reality where all races are one in Christ. Such a church may be a critical missional testimony to the world that the love of Christ can set people free.

Notes

1 See Dudley Baines, *Emigration from Europe, 1815–1930*, New Studies in Economic and Social History (New York: Cambridge University Press, 1995).

2 Phil Wood and Charles Landry, *The Intercultural City: Planning for Diversity Advantage* (London: Earthscan, 2008), p. 26.

3 Stephen Jivraj, *How Has Ethnic Diversity Grown 1991–2001–2011?*, (Manchester: University of Manchester, 2012).

4 Richard T. Pascale, Mark Millemann and Linda Gioja, *Surfing the Edge of Chaos: The Laws of Nature and the New Laws of Business* (New York: Crown Business, 2000), p. 20.

5 Pascale, Millemann and Gioja, *Surfing*, pp. 20–21.

6 Hanciles, *Beyond Christendom: Globalization, African Migration, and the Transformation of the West*, pp. 316–23. Also see Charles Taylor and Amy Gutmann, *Multiculturalism: Examining the Politics of Recognition* (Princeton, NJ: Princeton University Press, 1994).

7 Most notable voices announcing the failure of multiculturalism in Europe include Angela Merkel (Germany), David Cameron (Britain), Vladimir Putin (Russia) and Nicolas Sarkozy (France). See Will Kymlicka, 'Multiculturalism: Success, Failure, and the Future' (Washington DC: Migration Policy Institute, 2012).

8 Stephen Castles and Mark J. Miller, *The Age of Migration: International Population Movements in the Modern World*, 4th edn (New York: Guilford Press, 2009).

9 United Nations Migration Report, www.un.org/en/development/desa/popu lation/migration/data/estimates2/estimates19.asp (accessed 30.9.19).

10 Mark Chaves, *Congregations in America* (Cambridge, MA: Harvard University Press, 2004).

11 Charles Taylor, 'The Politics of Recognition', in Amy Gutmann (ed.), *Multiculturalism: Examining the Politics of Recognition* (Princeton, NJ: Princeton University Press, 1994), p. 38.

12 Taylor, 'The Politics of Recognition', p. 38.

13 Taylor, 'The Politics of Recognition', p. 38.

14 Taylor, 'The Politics of Recognition', p. 59.

15 Taylor, 'The Politics of Recognition', p. 66.

16 Gerald A. Arbuckle, *Earthing the Gospel: An Inculturation Handbook for Pastoral Workers* (Maryknoll, NY: Orbis, 1990), p. 181.

6

Diversity is a Terrible Thing to Waste

We have a proverb in Malawi, *mlendo ndi uyo abwera ndi kalumo kakuthwa*, which roughly translates as 'a guest usually comes with a sharp penknife'. The penknife was once considered the super-practical all-purpose tool used to resolve all kinds of challenges blocking a community's way to progress. It represents any tool that can be used to disentangle a community from its struggles and challenges. The penknife represents a new wisdom and understanding – a fresh set of eyes, a foreign perspective and a new way of looking at things – that may help the community solve its long-standing problems or make possible new opportunities. Like a penknife, the wisdom is hidden; we may not know it is there until it is needed and asked for. This penknife is sharper than the community's own penknives and can therefore cut through issues that have not been dealt with before. That is what a foreign perspective can do.

For the communities where these proverbs originated, access to fresh ideas, especially from outside, meant survival when hunger, diseases or even enemies struck, and that learning novel ideas from others could enhance the community's collective wisdom and help it negotiate many challenges. A community that does not encourage a heterogeneity of ideas is doomed to fail, as another Malawian proverb suggests – *nzeru zayekha anaviyika nsima mmadzi* interpreted – 'a person who believes he knows it all soaked his food in water because he could not ask how to get it out of its wrap'.

Homogeneity, whatever form it takes, is slow death. A community that builds walls to keep strangers out only imprisons itself within its own walls in the end. A prison guard is also a prisoner.

The Christian population in Britain now reflects the diversity that shapes the variegated body of Christ worldwide. This cultural diversity within the Christian community cannot be overemphasized, since it is possible to find Christians from every major people group in our cities. Now that we have this diversity of races, worldviews, theologies, cultures, what shall we do with it? Unfortunately, cultural diversity is often ignored – our congregations are shaped in ways that amplify the voices of one culture, be it African, British, Polish or American. I believe that humanity thrives only in the context of hospitality and generosity – one that is welcoming to the stranger. The absence of hospitality and generosity brings about isolation of both the guest and the host, and therefore diminishes life.

The cultural diversity we see in British Christianity is a gift from God. We can meet Christians from all over the world in our cities. Like the guest who brings a sharp penknife, they come bearing gifts that could invigorate British Christianity and help re-evangelize the nation. To reap its benefits, it may be helpful to be intentional in our response. A network of churches in the Midlands, for example, committed to embrace diversity a few years ago. They have made significant progress, and say that what has been critical for them was a commitment to include as many cultural voices in their decision-making systems as possible. When faced with the challenge of a rising Muslim population around some of their churches, they allowed their African leaders to instigate efforts to build bridges with their new neighbours. Many of those Africans grew up with Muslim neighbours and some have Muslims in their families, which made their efforts relatively easy. It is for reasons like these that I believe that cultural diversity is a terrible thing to waste.

So far, I have attempted to make a two-fold argument. First, I have suggested that unlike any other religion, Christianity today has a worldwide reach. It *finally* has followers among all major people groups in the world. It has been a slow journey that has taken 2,000 years but, finally God's vision of a worldwide body of disciples of Christ is almost possible. We can today find followers of Christ in every country in the world. Christians from around the world not only look different from each other, they also speak differently from one another. As a matter of fact, it is an advantage that they are different from one another in the ways they express their worship and do their theologies. Their Christianities are shaped in different cultural contexts, and they worship and theologize differently. Yet all Christians, regardless of where in the world they live, are brothers and sisters in Christ. As Christians, we belong to one kingdom – the *kingdom of our God*. We are all welcome to God's kingdom with our unique cultures. Being in the kingdom of God does not erase our cultural differences. To do so would be colonialism, and God does not colonize. Instead, the kingdom of God encourages all cultures to coexist while challenging them all (often through their intercultural encounters) to measure up to the image of the Son of God. The kingdom of God finds its fullest expression in intercultural mutuality. It is a multicultural kingdom. I have argued that God wanted it that way; God designed the kingdom to be multicultural. The Spirit of God that is poured upon all flesh establishes unity in diversity, and because of this we get to see God better when multiple cultures contribute to the image.

Second, I have argued that here in the West we have a great opportunity to preview a microcosm of the worldwide multicultural kingdom of God as expressed in our cities. Unlike scattered Christian communities worldwide who may have limited access to cultures beyond their own, we enjoy a variety of cultures in our Christian circles. Christians from all around the world are here in our cities. We do not need to go to Kenya to meet Kenyan Christians, or to go to Peru to meet Peruvian Christians. All we need to do is to cross the street in any British city and we will meet them. Brazilian Christians, Zimbabwean Christians, Nigerian Christians, they are all here in large numbers. Indeed, if Paul were to send an epistle to 'all (the saints) who are in London' (see Rom. 1.4) today, he would have to consider for his audience – as well as the British Christians in the city – Ethiopian, Nigerian, Syrian, Iranian, Brazilian Christians, and many others. The same could be said of any major European, American or Australian city. If it were possible for all Christians in any of our cities to get together in one place for a few hours, the fellowship we would enjoy on that one occasion would reveal just a small glimpse of what the worldwide body of Christ looks like. A snapshot of such a gathering would include people of all races, with their various skin colours and shades, speaking in many different languages and with numerous accents. It would be a lame and imperfect preview of the gathering of worshippers before the throne that John describes in Revelation 7, but it would still show us what heaven will be like. Such a multicultural event could bring together Africans, Asians, Latin Americans, Australians and many others to worship together. Just like in Acts 2, we could hear people speak of the great things God has done in Afrikaans, Bemba, Chewa, Dutch, Ewe, all the way to Zulu and beyond. We are living in a *kairotic* season, and it calls for wisdom – for people who understand the times and know what the Church ought to do.

In this chapter, I will highlight the significance of the opportunities that come with this new cultural diversity. I will argue that the cultural diversity we enjoy in the Christian community in the West is a gift from God that we need to celebrate and utilize for the sake of the kingdom. I am convinced that wherever communities are made up of people of different cultures, Christian churches must reflect that diversity in their gatherings. I say this for two reasons. First, the Scriptures seem to suggest that Christianity right from its beginnings has been a multicultural religion. Second, and following from the first, Christianity needs diversity if it is to reflect both the true image of the Son of God (who is revealed in diverse ways among God's people) and the communion of the Trinitarian God who has called us into the divine fellowship. Essentially, this blessing of cultural diversity that God has given us is a terrible thing to waste.

The Jewish diaspora of the first century CE

The mission of Jesus was to the entire world. However, to reach the world, he had to start somewhere: in a real-life context, Palestine, in a backyard area around the northern end of the Sea of Galilee. God's work in the nation of Israel had made the way for the Lord. Among the men and women of Galilee he had a platform: there was an expectation among Jews that a long-promised Messiah would come. Jesus came as that Messiah and on this premise – that he was the Messiah – he gathered his disciples (John 1.40), all of whom were Jewish even though the mission was to touch the ends of the earth. He then spent over three years travelling with them up and down the country, teaching them to save 'the lost sheep of the house of Israel' (Matt. 15.24), before they were to embark on a mission to save the world. Saving the lost sheep of Israel was his immediate focus, which was to serve as a training project for the disciples. This understanding of his mission led to what has been called the limited commission, in which Jesus instructed his disciples, 'Do not go into the way of the Gentiles, and do not enter a city of the Samaritans' (Matt. 10.5–6). In fact, Luke tells us that the limited commission took place in two phases. The first one is as recorded in Matthew 10 and Luke 9, while in the second phase Jesus appointed 'seventy others, and sent them two by two', again to the lost sheep of Israel (Luke 10.1). Their ministry would be limited to the house of Israel. However, as his ministry drew to a close, its focus changed and Jesus began to talk about reaching the nations. The limited commission was replaced by the great commission: Jesus now sent the disciples to all nations. Matthew 28.19 tells us that as Jesus prepared to go, he said to his disciples, 'Go therefore and make disciples of all nations, baptizing them in the name of the Father and of the Son and of the Holy Spirit, and teaching them to obey everything that I have commanded you. And remember, I am with you always, to the end of the age.' This is the *telos* of the three years of hard work: a community of disciples were now prepared to take on the nations. But were they ready?

Jewish diaspora as God's missional assets

The timings of God's work are always multidimensional. It is always best to look at the wider context of history to recognize some of God's background work that may not seem obvious. It helps us to understand the emergence of Christianity when we look at how God prepared the scene for it. Before Jesus came on the scene, God had been setting the stage for the world-transforming movement that he would initiate. The event of Jesus' life and mission is of such utmost importance, it required thorough preparation. There are various ways in which we can see God creating a perfect context for the mission of Jesus. The whole of Jewish history was pointing to the arrival of Jesus as the Messiah, so in a way all Jewish history thus far was God preparing the stage for Jesus. However, for our conversation, the two outstanding ways in which we see God preparing for the mission of Jesus are migration – especially the scattering of the Jews from Palestine to the wider world of the Roman empire and the Middle East and beyond – and the cultural diversity of the Roman empire. The birth and spread of Christianity would ride upon these two factors, and because of them we have world Christianity today.

By the time Jesus was born, Jewish people had gone through a series of dispersions from Palestine, and Jewish diaspora communities had emerged in the wider world beyond the Mediterranean basin and the Greco-Roman territories. For several centuries since the Assyrian dispersion (722 BCE) and the Babylonian captivity (597 BCE) there had been a constant movement of Jews away from the promised land. While many of them returned in waves from Babylon during the Persian period, a sizeable Jewish population remained in Mesopotamia. By the third century BCE, as Greek influence spread, Jewish communities continued to mushroom across the empire. The Greek diaspora prompted further Jewish diaspora. Both the Greeks and the Romans moved thousands of Jewish soldiers to towns outside Palestine. Large Jewish communities emerged in Antioch and Damascus, in the Phoenician ports and in the Asia Minor cities of Sardis, Halicarnassus, Pergamum and Ephesus. In 63 BCE, Pompey carried hundreds of Jews to Rome to be sold as slaves. The Ptolemies brought many Jewish soldiers to Egypt and in so doing increased the population of Jews in Egypt. Alexandria would become home to the largest number of Jews outside Palestine. It was the Jews of Alexandria who translated the Old Testament from Hebrew to Greek, completing the Septuagint in 132 BCE. Eventually, the Jews scattered inland, beyond the Mediterranean coast and up the Nile valley, resulting in a very strong Jewish presence all the way to Nubia in the first century CE. Philo, a Jewish philosopher of Alexandria, once commented that 'Jews in Alexandria and Egypt from the Libyan slope to the borders of Aethiopia do not fall short of a million', and that 'no single country can contain the Jews because of their multitude'. A Greek geographer by the name of Strabo is recorded to have said at the end of the first century BCE, 'you can't go anywhere in the civilized world without encountering a Jew'.

By the time we come to Acts 2 when the Church is born in Jerusalem, the Jewish diaspora was quite large and influential. Jews lived on most of the islands of the eastern Mediterranean (such as Cyprus and Crete), in mainland Greece and Macedonia, on the shores of the Black Sea, and in the Balkans, in Rome and throughout the Italian peninsula, Egypt, Libya, and as far west in North Africa as Carthage. Luke takes the trouble to list those that there were present in Jerusalem for the Feast of Pentecost 'devout Jews from every nation under heaven … Parthians, Medes and Elamites; residents of Mesopotamia, Judea and Cappadocia, Pontus and Asia, Phrygia and Pamphylia, Egypt and the parts of Libya near Cyrene; visitors from Rome (both Jews and converts to Judaism); Cretans and Arabs' (Acts 2.9–11). All these diaspora Jews witnessed the event of the pouring out of the Spirit that day and would take the news about it to their towns long before the missionaries arrived. They would tell – in their synagogues all around the known world then – of the strange thing that happened in Jerusalem: 'we heard them speaking in our own tongues the wonderful works of God'. This would prepare, even in a small way, for the time when the gospel would be preached in their cities.

Within a few decades of Pentecost, there would be more Jews living in the diaspora than in Judah. After 70 CE, when the Romans destroyed the Temple in Jerusalem and deported many Jews to Syria, Asia Minor, Italy and other parts of the empire, even more Jewish communities sprang up in every large city of the empire, from the Persian Gulf in the east to Spain in the west. With the temple destroyed, there was not much to go back to and so the diaspora became home. By the end of the first century CE, Jews were effectively diffused throughout the Roman empire. This extensive presence of Jewish diaspora communities at the time when Christianity was emerging would play a significant role in its spread.

As a matter of fact, as the Church was emerging in the first chapters of Acts, the diaspora Jews also helped its establishment in Jerusalem. It was diaspora Jews who helped transition the Jesus movement from Galilee to Jerusalem. This transition was geographical but, more important, it was political. Jesus had taken a group of men from a small geographical space on the northern shore of the Sea of Galilee, in a remote part of the distant Roman province of Judea, and left them the responsibility of preaching in Jerusalem, Judea, Samaria, to the ends of the earth. There was a problem, in that Galileans were practically inferior foreigners in Jerusalem. Judean Jews despised Galilean Jews; Galileans were thought to be culturally and religiously second class. The Galileans also had a distinctive rural accent that easily betrayed them as foreigners in Jerusalem. When Peter denied Christ he was identified by his Galilean accent (Matt. 26.73). Even when they preached in places like Rome, they were ridiculed for their accent. Jesus' origins in Nazareth (earning him the name Jesus of Nazareth) played right into the socio-political scene of first-century Palestine. It was not just a riddle when Nathanael asked, 'Can anything good come out of Nazareth?' The Pharisees of John 7.52 stated, wrongly, that no prophet had ever risen out of Galilee.

The promotion of the movement from Galilee to Jerusalem (and later to the nations) could only happen with the help of diaspora Jews. The most obvious example is Mary the mother of John Mark (John Mark is generally agreed to be the writer of the second Gospel). Mary and her family had lived for a long time in Cyrene, Libya, where Mark was born. They had returned to Jerusalem where they had a large house, in which was the Upper Room (of the Last Supper and the post-Ascension hiding/waiting) and to which Peter went after being released from prison by an angel. Most likely, Mary's house continued to serve as a fellowship space for the early Church. Both John Mark and his cousin Barnabas, another diaspora Jew from Cyprus, would be influential in taking the gospel beyond Jerusalem. Another example of the role of diaspora Jews in Jerusalem comes in Acts 6 when there was a need for a new tier of leaders in the Church. The apostles asked the church to 'seek out from among them seven men of good reputation, full of the Holy Spirit and wisdom' (Acts 6.3). They chose Stephen, Philip, Prochorus, Nicanor, Timon, Parmenas, and Nicholas (a proselyte from Antioch). All these names are Greek, suggesting that they were diaspora Jews.

Diaspora Jews would have even more impact in the spread of Christianity outside Palestine. First, by the time the Church emerged, they had established networks of synagogues wherever they lived. Synagogues were primarily places where Jewish communities gathered for public worship and religious instruction, but they also served secular functions such as political gatherings, providing accommodation to travelling Jews, courts for administering justice. When Christian missionaries travelled in the diaspora, the synagogues made a natural contact point for the gospel. For instance, Luke's narrative in Acts depicts Paul attempting to evangelize the Jewish diaspora in the synagogues first when he arrived at a new place. We see Paul first preaching in the synagogue of Damascus (Acts 9.20); Pisidian Antioch (Acts 13.14), Iconium (Acts 14.1), Philippi (Acts 16.13), Thessalonica (Acts 17.1–2), Berea (Acts 17.10), Athens

(Acts 17.17), Corinth (Acts 18.4–6) and Ephesus (Acts 18.19; 19.8). In Pisidian Antioch, Paul declares that he would 'now turn to the Gentiles' (Acts 13.46) because the Jews rejected the gospel, but we see him continue to address fellow Jews first in synagogues (Acts 18.4–6, 19; 19.8).

Second, because of the prevalent presence of Jews in various parts of the Greco-Roman world, there emerged a Gentile population of proselytes and God-fearers. Both these groups were Gentiles who were attracted to Judaism, only differing in how they responded to it. Proselytes converted to Judaism, submitting themselves to circumcision in the process. God-fearers were sympathetic to Judaism, and generally agreed with the ethical monotheism of the Jews; they attended Jewish synagogue services but did not commit to the point of being circumcised or to the observance of the Torah in its entirety. Both proselytes and God-fearers furnished the spread of the gospel, serving as a bridge between the Jews and the Gentiles around them. Cornelius was a God-fearer who was converted together with his household in Acts 10. Lydia (Acts 16) was a God-fearer from Asia Minor. She and her household became Paul's first converts to Christianity in Europe in the town of Philippi. I should add here that some scholars believe that Luke, author of the Gospel and Acts of the Apostles, was also a diasporic Jew from Antioch. He was a disciple of Paul's and travelled with him extensively. Luke contributed 25 per cent of the New Testament; Luke and Paul together wrote 50 per cent of the New Testament.

Third, in Acts 11, when Jewish Christians fled from persecution in Jerusalem, Luke tells us that it was the diaspora Jews who made the commitment to break with tradition to evangelize Gentiles. This was a radical move that required courage – it is told to us right after the story of Peter's conversion to the Gentile cause after his encounter with Cornelius, and if there is anything that Luke wants us to understand in that narrative, it is that Peter is very apologetic about preaching to a Gentile. He does his best to make everyone understand that all this is done on God's initiative. He has nothing to do with it. It took God four attempts to convince Peter that he could not call unclean something that God had called clean. If anyone had problems with the fact that a Roman centurion had been saved, they had to take it up with God. In the same spirit, Palestinian (non-diasporic) Jews were neither ready nor willing to evangelize Gentiles when they fled Jerusalem. It was the Hellenistic Jews who took the lead. When a congregation emerged in Antioch, the leaders in Jerusalem sent Barnabas, a Hellenistic Jew from Cyprus, to go to Antioch. Convinced that it was God's work, Barnabas brought Paul, another Hellenistic Jew, from Tarsus to help lead the work. A year later, the Spirit directed the congregation to send their key leaders, Barnabas and Saul – two diaspora

83

didn't jesus talk about this during his time w(them?

Jews – to go on a trip to serve God among the Gentiles. The implications of the decision in Acts 11 to evangelize Gentiles would only be ratified at the Council of Jerusalem in Acts 15. Those diaspora Jews permanently changed the Church.

Multicultural witness

The Mediterranean basin in the first century had people from many cultures living together and interacting on a constant basis. It was a world in which cultural diversity was normative, especially in the cities and towns. Roman rule created a multiculturalism that forced various nationalities to coexist in its cities. People were allowed, and actually encouraged, to migrate around the empire – often settling in urban centres of the empire that, at the time, comprised a third of the world's population and extended far beyond the Mediterranean area. Thus, every major town and city had people from different parts of the world living together. Cities such as Alexandria, Antioch, Ephesus, Corinth and Rome were all multicultural melting pots with communities of people from Africa, Asia and Europe living together. Even Palestine, the primary setting of the Gospels, being a colony of Rome was also home to Gentiles from around the empire and beyond. Indeed, Galilee was 'Galilee of the nations' because of the many ethnicities who had lived there for centuries by the time of the New Testament. Jerusalem, the religious centre of the Jews, drew people from the wider world beyond the Mediterranean and the Middle East. This is the world that shaped early Christianity and gave it its identity.

The multiculturalism of the empire also allowed for various religions to thrive together. Christianity emerged into a context of religious pluralism, and Judaism was not its only competitor. Many Romans practised the imperial cult, worshipping the emperor in addition to countless other pagan gods that were popular around the empire. The Greeks had a long tradition of religious systems that continued long after their civilization had disappeared. Some Greek gods are mentioned in the Bible. For instance, in Acts 14, Paul and Barnabas are mistaken for the Greek gods Zeus and Hermes. In Acts 19, we hear of Artemis, the patron god of Ephesus. In Acts 28, Luke mentions Dioskouroi, which actually referred to the twin sailor-gods Castor and Polydeuces, who were believed to be sons of Zeus. Paul's sermon at the Areopagus (Acts 17) was delivered in response to the fact that he saw that the city (of Athens) was 'given over to idols' (Acts 17.16). On the other side of the Mediterranean, the Egyptians worshipped their own gods, among them being the sun and the Nile. Christianity did not come into a religious vacuum. In the multicultural cities, people practised the religions of their communities. Thus, even though people lived together across cultures, their religious lives were segregated. The Romans and the Greeks worshipped their own gods in their own communities. The Egyptians worshipped their Egyptian gods and the Jews worshipped in their synagogues. It was the Christian communities that attracted people of different cultural backgrounds and national identities to worship the newfound Jewish Messiah, also known as the Way, the Nazarene, the *Christos* (Messiah, Anointed One) and the *kurios* (Lord) for the Greeks and the Romans.

Nevertheless, beneath this beautiful image of multicultural cities of people from various parts of the empire and religious traditions, we know that there was a deep-seated segregation between classes, races and every possible dividing line. Pious Jews did not mix with Gentiles; slaves had to avoid any form of social association with their masters; and women were second-class citizens. People of many cultures lived in close proximity and yet there was great segregation in the ways they interacted. Society was stratified in a hierarchy, separated according to ethnicity, economic capacity and sexuality. Of course, race, money and sex have always driven the human race and are as such easily used to divide and marginalize the haves from the have-nots. The Greeks looked down upon the barbarians as uncivilized while the Jews despised the Greeks as the uncircumcised (the term Greek itself would come to mean 'Gentile'). The Romans sat at the top of the pecking order as the colonizers of the entire Mediterranean region, lording it over both Jews and Greeks. In addition, citizens (which often meant free men) were socially higher than the slaves they owned and actually needed in order to be effective citizens. Women were placed towards the bottom of the hierarchy. Indeed, a typical Hellenistic man's morning prayer at the time involved thanking God that he was made Greek and not a Barbarian, a citizen and not a slave, and a man not a woman. This prayer also appears in Judaism and can still be found in some Jewish cycles of morning prayer:

Blessed art thou, O Lord our God, King of the universe,
who hast not made me a foreigner.
Blessed art thou, O Lord our God, King of the universe,
who hast not made me a slave.
Blessed art thou, O Lord our God, King of the Universe,
who hast not made me a woman.

Neither Jew nor Greek

Christian communities, unlike these other religions, attracted members from different cultural groups. They brought Jews and Gentiles together to worship a Jewish Messiah whose mission was no longer only to the lost house of Israel but to the entire world. Among the Gentiles joining this new fellowship were people from around the empire. They would all change their religious habits. They gathered on the first day of the week and not on the sabbath. They worshipped Jesus and not the emperor or any of their cultural gods. Jews and Gentiles ate together, as long as the Gentiles would not bring food offered to idols to the table. Thus, these new fellowships were a radical change from the regimented and segregated social and religious life of the first-century Greco-Roman world. Because of the unique multicultural nature of these communities, they needed a new identifier. In Antioch they were first called *christianoi* to mark them as being different from any other religious groups around.

The Antioch church seems to have been very multicultural. Perhaps they had no choice. They lived in a multicultural city; they were evangelizing both their Jewish and Gentile neighbours, and they were committed to avoiding segregated fellowships. A multicultural fellowship was a natural outcome of their sense of mission and evangelism as well as of their context. Luke's list of the leadership team in the new church in Antioch is as multicultural as you can get: Saul, a diaspora Jew from Tarsus, Simeon, also called the Niger because he was black-skinned and most likely an African, Lucius, probably a diaspora Jew from Cyrene in Libya, therefore an African, and Barnabas, a diaspora Jew from Cyprus.

Paul was most likely the theologian-in-residence in Antioch and is especially informative on the theological underpinnings of a multicultural worship community as he discusses the implications of the baptism into Christ in his letter to the new Gentile Christians in the town of Galatia.

> For in Christ Jesus you are all children of God through faith. As many of you as were baptized into Christ have clothed yourselves with Christ. There is no longer Jew or Greek, there is no longer slave or free, there is no longer male and female; for all of you are one in Christ Jesus. And if you belong to Christ, then you are Abraham's offspring, heirs according to the promise. (Gal. 3.26–29)

He goes against the three key opposing distinctions: ethnicity, social status and gender. Paul himself had most likely cited these three distinctions in prayer before he came to the faith; now, he challenges them knowing that all three had considerable importance in Judaism, and

how do you reach those who are on the higher end?

affirms that in Christ they are all irrelevant. His argument is not only theoretical or imaginary, as some would like to believe. He wrote his epistle to a genuine community in which these distinctions and the segregation they produced were real. He was most certainly concerned with practical church life in congregations where men and women, Jews and Gentiles, slaves and free persons were fellow members. The multicultural city did not overcome segregation. To a great extent, the cultural diversity revealed – as it does today – the deep-rooted human tendencies to box, segregate and discriminate. Consequently, as the Christian message spread from one city to another and wrestled with the social ills of the day, it had to challenge the problem of segregation. This is Paul's radical agenda here. The segregation that shaped the general society was not welcome in God's new *ekklesia*. Members of the emerging *one* body of Christ ought not to be segregated into Jewish churches against Greek churches, free churches against slave churches, or male churches against female churches. Once new followers are baptized into Christ, they cannot practise segregation. Baptism often involved derobing new converts of old garments, immersing them in water and then robing them with new garments. Paul is suggesting here that the new garment is Christ – Jesus becomes our new primary identity. The simple event of baptism qualifies everyone to become children of God and brings them together into the body of Christ by the unity of the Spirit. Everyone cloaked in this new garment (Jews, Gentiles, slaves, free people, men and women) has been made into one new humanity that identifies with Christ so irreducibly that they have basically become one person. Members of the Church have become one and been taken into the corpus of Christ. Everyone who has been baptized as a follower of Christ, no matter their ethnic, social or sexual distinctions, is welcome as a full member of the Church. Christ had become the marginalized slave on their behalf so that they could become full citizens in the *ekklesia*.

Paul first challenges the religious and ethnic distinction that existed between Jews and Greeks (by which he also means Gentiles). The religious order of the day made the Jew the first-class citizen, not only in Palestine but also in other Jewish-dominated areas (apparently including Galatia). Jews believed themselves to be the chosen people who worshipped the real God and thus needed to keep themselves socially separate. They had religious and social rights and privileges that Gentiles did not have, and needed to preserve them from Gentile contamination. Jesus referred to this Jewish exclusiveness in his discourse at the well with the woman of Samaria (John 4). After a somewhat lengthy exchange, the climax of the conversation comes when Jesus declares to the woman that 'we [Jews] worship what we do know, for salvation is from the Jews' (v. 22). This comes after telling her, 'You [Gentiles] worship what you do not know' (v. 22). However, the heart of the matter is that Jesus, being a Jewish man, broke with tradition when he asked for water from a Gentile woman. No wonder the woman hesitates, asking Jesus, 'How is it that you, being a Jew, ask a drink of me, a woman of Samaria?' (John 4.9). In that world, Gentiles – which included all non-Jews – were second-class citizens, the Samaritans, who were half-cousins to the Jews. The Samaritan woman's life circumstances would make her even less than second class. Nevertheless, Jesus' conversation with her points towards a future when Jews and Gentiles, as a new humanity, would worship together in Spirit and truth. Paul suggests in Galatians that the day is come, for in the new fellowship of the Spirit, Jews and Gentiles belong together in unity.

Second, for this new community of the followers of Christ, Paul declares null and void the social and economic distinction that kept citizens from mixing with slaves. Citizens enjoyed the free life, organizing the matters of the city in the assembly, while slaves worked long hours out in the elements producing goods that would provide for the families of the citizens. Indeed, slaves kept the economy going. The economic system depended on them and thus demanded that slaves be kept in their place at the bottom of the social hierarchy. Without them the entire civilization was in danger. Slaves were totally dependent on their masters for their livelihood. They were the ultimate second-class citizens, with no rights of their own. Paul challenges this and declares that in Christ there is neither free nor slave. Masters and slaves were brothers and sisters in Christ. The economic stratification of society that separates the haves from the have-nots and leaves the latter at the mercy of the former is also not welcome in the body of Christ. He further clarifies this in 1 Corinthians 7.22 where he says, 'For whoever was called in the Lord as a slave is a freed person belonging to the Lord, just as whoever was free when called is a slave of Christ.' He later instructs Christian masters and Christian slaves to relate to one another in a way that is informed by their mutual faith and service to Christ (Col. 3.22—4.1). However, the most telling implication of baptism was that slaves and free persons became one in Christ.

The third division that Paul demolishes is that between male and female members of society. The culture that shaped the New Testament is evidently steeped in patriarchy. Men have power over everyone and everything around them while women are often portrayed as powerless and limited in many ways. Women were treated as second-class citizens whose main role in life was to make the livelihoods of men more pleasurable. This distinction, too, is not welcome in the body of Christ.

One new humanity

Essentially, Paul is suggesting that the Galatians' baptism into Christ ought to make them realize that these distinctions – ethnicity, social and sexual – no longer exist and their non-existence makes it possible for all to participate not only in Christ's death but also in Christ's resurrection, forming a new humanity in Christ. All the old dividing walls are demolished. Everything has become new. Those who have been baptized in Christ have put off their former selves. The old humanity is gone – a new humanity has come. Something radical happened within the baptized community so that 'there was neither Jew nor Greek, slave or free, male or female'. These distinctions have been permanently changed or superseded; through baptism they enter into a new relationship with Christ and become 'all one in Christ Jesus'. They stand completely new and in a different relationship to the world. The racial, social and sexual distinctions of before are covered up by the new garment they receive – Christ. These distinctions have been transcended in Christ. There is only one body and one Spirit.

> For as in one body we have many members, and not all the members have the same function, so we, who are many, are one body in Christ, and individually we are members one of another. We have gifts that differ according to the grace given to us: prophecy, in proportion to faith; ministry, in ministering; the teacher, in teaching; the exhorter, in exhortation; the giver, in generosity; the leader, in diligence; the compassionate, in cheerfulness. (Rom. 12.4–8)

The Spirit of God, in God's wisdom and plan, gives gifts to members (or parts) of the body of the Son that are now, in a literal sense, dispersed around the world. No one part has all the gifts, yet the whole body needs all the gifts. If one part lacks anything, the whole body is lacking. While Paul might have had one particular congregation or church in Rome in mind, this Scripture speaks to the worldwide body of Christ's disciples. Most certainly, he did not think of one congregation to be a full body of Christ for there is only one body (Eph. 4.4). All Christian communities around the world together form the body of Christ. They are all members of one body. However, as members of the body scattered around the world, they are gifted differently, yet in a complementary manner, according to God's grace, and those parts who have the gifts are required to share them with other parts who have different gifts. The African Church has been given gifts that the worldwide Church needs and, of course, the worldwide Church has gifts that the African Church needs. The same applies to Asian, Latin American, European and American churches. Within any nation, local and foreign Christians carry gifts for one another – gifts that not only make the body more whole if shared and received, but also bring Christians closer together so that they can access and enjoy each other's gifts. Churches from different parts of the world bring gifts that they each need from one another. The body will function better if every member does its part by bringing its gifts to the table.

For us here in Britain, migrant Christians bring gifts that British churches need to receive, and British churches have gifts that migrant Christians need. For the body to be whole, it needs the gifts of all churches to be fully contributed. Paul urges those with the different gifts (such as prophecy, faith, ministry and teaching) to use them for the edification of the body. In his first letter to the Corinthians, Paul adds:

> For just as the body is one and has many members, and all the members of the body, though many, are one body, so it is with Christ. For in the one Spirit we were all baptized into one body – Jews or Greeks, slaves or free – and we were all made to drink of one Spirit. Indeed, the body does not consist of one member but of many. If the foot were to say, 'Because I am not a hand, I do not belong to the body', that would not make it any less a part of the body. And if the ear were to say, 'Because I am not an eye, I do not belong to the body', that would not make it any less a part of the body. If the whole body were an eye, where would the hearing be? If the whole body were hearing, where would the sense of smell be? But as it is, God arranged the members in the body, each one of them, as he chose. If all were a single member, where would the body be? As it is, there are many members, yet one body. The eye cannot say to the hand, 'I have no need of you', nor again the head to the feet, 'I have no need of you.' On the contrary, the members of the body that seem to be weaker are indispensable, and those members of the body that we think less honourable we clothe with greater honour, and our less respectable members are treated with greater respect; whereas our more respectable members do not need this. But God has so arranged the body, giving the greater honour to the inferior member, that there may be no dissension within the body, but the members may have the same care for one another. If one member suffers, all suffer together with it; if one member is honoured, all rejoice together with it. Now you are the body of Christ and individually members of it. (1 Cor. 12.12–27)

This rather lengthy quotation highlights the point that this book is trying to make: British churches cannot say to African churches, 'We have no need of you.' Neither can African churches say to Asian churches, 'We can do without you.' As a matter of fact, no church should be able to dismiss any other church as non-essential, just as much as one member of the human body cannot say to another part, 'You are of no use to me.' In the grand scheme of God's mission – which requires a functional body of Christ here on earth – all parts of the body need one another. Their mutual exchange of gifts enriches all of them. Intercultural exchange is even more needful when migrant and local churches are located in the same city, trying to evangelize the same people. In Ephesians, Paul writes:

> The whole body [is] joined and knit together by what every joint supplies, according to the effective working by which every part does its share, causes growth of the body for the edifying of itself in love. (Eph. 4.16, NKJV)

Or, as the NRSV reads:

> from whom the whole body, joined and knit together by every ligament with which it is equipped, as each part is working properly, promotes the body's growth in building itself up in love.

The worldwide body of Christ is joined and knit together by the gifts that different members of the body bring. Each part must contribute. Paul beseeches the Ephesians to 'lead a life worthy of the calling ... with all humility and gentleness, with patience, bearing with one another in love, making every effort to maintain the unity of the Spirit in the bond of peace' (Eph. 4.1–3). He foresees cross-cultural miscommunications, racial divisions and other forces of evil that would want them separated, and yet he encourages them to do whatever they can to keep the body together.

I believe that the gifts that migrant Christians bring when they migrate can help reinvigorate British Christianity. As such, it is best to engage one another by first listening both to each other and to God about the gifts that both bring. Instead of first focusing on how our differences should pull us apart, we might seek to discern how those differences (and our different gifts) can bring us together and help us both in our journey in God's mission in our neighbourhoods and in the world at large. Difference is not the enemy; the fear of difference is. There will be differences in our theologies, ecclesiologies, liturgies, for example, but instead of trying to iron out the differences – to achieve some kind of uniformity – we can focus on what we can learn from one another and how best we can receive the gifts of the other in order to achieve <u>unity in diversity</u>. To put it in a more missional way, maybe we could focus on what God is saying to us or teaching us through the presence of the strangers among us. This is a two-way process: both migrant and British churches will learn from the other.

Theologies

The rise of different expressions of Christianity around the world has led to the emergence of theologies that are significantly different from those of the West. These foreign theologies in the non-Western world have often rejected the Western cultural baggage and theological hegemony that were exported with Western Christianity to the rest of the world. They are adamant that every theology that we hear is shaped by the context in which it emerges. Consequently, every theology is a contextual theology, being focused on answering questions and addressing the concerns of the people among whom it emerges. As such, it cannot fully – or *really* – answer questions being asked elsewhere. No theology is supposed to be universal – to be relevant in all places at all times.

It should be expected, then, that the theologies of foreign Christians in Britain will in some aspects be remarkably different from British theologies, and from one another. Asian theology, born in Asian culture, will be radically different from Latin American theology and African theology. Even in Britain, a theology that responds to the concerns of Londoners will be different from a theology that speaks to fishing communities along the Scottish coast. While Africans, for instance, may know very little about ancient theologians such as Augustine, and even less of Karl Barth, that is not necessarily a bad thing for them. This is maybe an area where Africans could receive the gifts brought by Western Christians, as even though Augustine and Karl Barth do not attend to the many issues that African Christians have to face on a daily basis like poverty, political corruption and witchcraft, they speak of God in ways that Africans need to hear. What the Africans bring to the table is a vibrant spirit-centred worldview (or theology) that encourages them to pray hard, engage in spiritual warfare to wrestle with the spirit world and conduct exorcisms in order to liberate people from witchcraft and the oppression of the evil one – things that are distant to many Western Christians.

Foreign Christians bring their theologies with them when they migrate to Britain. It is a positive development that British Christianity is now coming into contact with foreign Christians and their theologies. This is perhaps God's doing; it may be the blessed reflex in action, helping British Christianity to listen to and learn from foreign Christians who have migrated from places that have had Christianity for only a few centuries. When British Christians engage with foreign Christians in theological conversations – with the intention of learning from one another, and not trying to teach and convert one another – both their theologies are enriched. The more we learn from one another, the better our understanding of God. As we progress through the twenty-first century, and as many British and non-Western Christians worship together, if only on the road to their segregated churches, it is important that Christian theology becomes a field where Western and non-Western theologians can engage one another in mutually critiquing and edifying conversations that enrich British Christianity. So far, theological tensions exist when African and Western Christians meet. Sometimes their reading of Scripture differs, and both groups become defensive. None of this is helpful. Both these groups need to slow down and engage each other in thoughtful conversations, listening to what God may be saying through the other. Such conversations are good for the entire enterprise of theology – a field whose global voices desperately need to change from a cacophony of theological arguments and misunderstandings to a polyphony of various theological voices and perspectives speaking to one another in harmony and humility, as they together celebrate the Spirit of God who speaks equally to Westerners and non-Westerners.

7

The Multicultural Imperative

At the heart of missional theology is the conviction that God is at work in the geographical and social context of every congregation. Missional congregations understand themselves to be participating in God's mission both locally and globally. Thus, it is rather surprising that both in Europe and in North America – continents that boast of cultural diversity – *missional* does not translate multicultural. Aylward Shorter suggests that 'Becoming a truly multicultural church is not a question of resolving cultural differences, or ironing out diversities ... It is much more an orientation to the future, a call to convergence, than a resolution of past divergences.'[1] Indeed, the future of Christianity looks like Joseph's robe of many colours. Some denominations will have to embrace diversity because of the need to survive, largely using assimilation to keep the colours in the ranks. Others will do it because of the missional call to be a prayer house for all nations. As the West becomes more multicultural, monocultural congregations will be increasingly difficult to justify.

Creation, in all its magnificence and splendour, testifies to God's love for diversity. From the myriad types of fish in the seas to the thousands of birds of the air, there is a huge multiplicity of species in the world. It is as if God created one species of something, saw it was good and went on to create millions upon millions of other species, just to enjoy variety. God created human beings and made sure that each one of them is unique. There are over 7 billion human beings in the world today, and none of us is exactly alike. We come in different shapes, sizes and skin colours, in thousands of ethnic groups and speaking even more thousands of languages and dialects. Cultures and traditional customs will vary from one ethnic group to the next. Musical interests and expressions, which for many people in the world are religious and spiritual phenomena, vary from one continent to another. Dressing styles, eating habits, philosophies and worldviews that shape people's understanding of life differ from place to place. Variety is what keeps the world going. The human race thrives because of continued mixing of the gene pool. Without enough variety, we would survive for only a few generations.

Trinitarian theology

The return of Trinitarian theology in the past century provides excellent justification for multiculturalism within the Church. The developing dialogue between Western theology and the Eastern Orthodox tradition becomes especially helpful here. The fact that Western theology takes time to hear what Eastern Orthodox theology has to offer is in itself a major move. And to prove the point, it is Eastern theology's understanding of the Trinity as social and relational that enhances the argument for multicultural congregations. Such an understanding makes room for a relationship with a different other. There has to be an 'other' for there to be a relationship, in the same way that there is the Father, the Son and the Spirit. John Zizioulas makes it explicit in his book *Communion and Otherness.*

> There is no model for the proper relation between communion and otherness either for the church or for the human being other than the Trinitarian God. If the church wants to be faithful to her true self, she must mirror the communion and otherness that exists in the Triune God ... The relation between communion and otherness in God is the model for both *ecclesiology* and *anthropology*.[2]

Zizioulas goes further to ground this communion with the other in the cruciform nature of the gospel. Communion with the other requires the experience of the cross.[3] It is possible only as we sacrifice our own wills both to God and to our neighbours, in a self-emptying way of the incarnation that is not determined by the qualities that the other possesses. 'We cannot discriminate between those who are and those who are not worthy of our acceptance.'[4] As a matter of fact, the Word testifies to the fact that when Jesus is glorified, he will draw all people unto himself.[5] The cross is essential to the coming together of *all* human beings to Christ. As Paul argues in Galatians, in Christ there are no racial distinctions. Greeks and Jews are equal before God. This 'all people' is a truly multicultural community created by the Spirit of God, not just an eschatological one.

Pneumatology

The Church in its global manifestations is an expression of the work of God's Spirit, the Spirit of the Father and the Spirit of Christ. This one Spirit is poured out upon all flesh, irrespective of ethnicity. This is one of the most disturbing facts about the Spirit, and has the most to teach us: the same Spirit is poured out on white Christians, black Christians, Hispanic Christians. We should be ready to receive of the Spirit in spite of the colour of the vessel. If we really believe that the same Spirit is operational in our white friends and in our black friends, we will be truly open to hearing what the Spirit has to say through the stranger.

On the Day of Pentecost, the disciples spoke with other tongues as the Spirit gave them utterance. Michael Welker suggests that two significant miracles occurred here. The first was that of speaking with other tongues, which other Jews from the diaspora were able to comprehend. The second, and according to Welker more profound, was that of hearing. Both these miracles are cross-cultural.

> Without dissolving the variety and complexity of their backgrounds, without setting aside their forms of expression and understanding ... an unbelievable commonality of experience and understanding occurs ... This is what is truly spectacular and shocking about the Pentecost event.[6]

Welker adds:

> The Pentecost event connects intense experiences of individuality with a new experience of community ... Instead, one's own particularity is experienced in the midst of a consciously perceived polyindividuality and polyconcreteness, in the midst of diversity which, while foreign to the individual human person, through the Pentecost event makes possible the commonality and common experience and language.[7]

The Spirit does not quash difference. Diversity becomes the basis of a vibrant community. Through the pouring out of the Spirit, God effects a world-encompassing, multilingual, polyindividual testimony of Godself. This polyindividual nature of the Christian community is what Miroslav Volf calls the catholic personality, 'a personality enriched by otherness, a personality which is what it is only because multiple others have been reflected in it in a particular way'.[8]

Paul testifies to this when he talks about the distribution of the charisms. Each member of the community is a necessary member of the body of Christ, with certain charisms. They are given to the members of the body of Christ, and to the Church as a whole, in ways that encourage interdependence and mutual edification. No one congregation, and no one culture, has them all. They ought to be shared among many.

The Spirit does not erase bodily inscribed differences, but allows access into the one body of Christ to the people with such differences on the same terms ... The gifts of the Spirit are given irrespective of such differences.[9]

In addition, it has to be said that part of my conviction as an African Charismatic Christian is that the Spirit of God is already at work in every culture. Craig Carter's critique of Richard Niebuhr's typologies in *Christ and Culture* agrees with this.[10]

Miroslav Volf adds: 'Each culture can retain its own cultural specificity ... Paul deprives each culture of ultimacy in order to give them all legitimacy in the wider family of cultures.'[11] He suggests that the Church should have a catholic cultural identity. 'Other cultures are not a threat to the pristine purity of our cultural identity, but a potential source of enrichment.'[12]

All this variety is God's idea and creation. God does not intend for us to be the same. God's Spirit does not ask us to be uniform. Surely, God does not expect us all to worship in the same manner. When Christ prays that we should be one, he does not mean that there should be no differences among us. Rather, he wants us to be united even though we are different. He wants us to be different but united. Christ does not expect Anglicans in Lagos to worship exactly like Anglicans in London. Our differences are God-given and God-ordained because God loves diversity. The Spirit creates the fellowship (or, in the words of Anglicans, the *communion*) to which we all – with our differences – belong. This global communion of Christ-followers is only possible if we commit to keeping the unity in our diversity. It is our unity that makes us the fellowship of the Spirit – the fellowship belonging to the Spirit. The Spirit of God is no author of confusion. It does not cause disunity. If we truly belong to the Spirit, we will be united even in our diversity. In addition, the Spirit's fellowship with us – its closeness alongside us – is made possible by – and therefore depends on – our unity. Strife, divisions and discord are of the devil and only serve to prevent us from the unity to which God calls us. People who have tasted this diverse yet united fellowship of the Spirit often say, 'Christ was the only common thing among us when we started out. We shared nothing but our faith in him. The Spirit kept us together, and now we are one large united family.'

This unity of the Spirit is especially critical when there are cultural and theological differences among us (which is quite often). The fact that we are a large body that finds expression in all major cultures in the world means that there will be cultural differences and various theological perspectives. It would not make sense to expect Congolese to worship or do

97

their theology like Germans, Brazilians, or even Americans. The Maori people of New Zealand will understand and worship God in ways that are different, and justifiably so, from those of the Maasai of Tanzania and Kenya. It is for this reason that Paul urges the Ephesians to keep the unity of the Spirit through the bond of peace.

> I therefore, the prisoner in the Lord, beg you to lead a life worthy of the calling to which you have been called, with all humility and gentleness, with patience, bearing with one another in love, making every effort to maintain the unity of the Spirit in the bond of peace. There is one body and one Spirit, just as you were called to the one hope of your calling, one Lord, one faith, one baptism, one God and Father of all, who is above all and through all and in all. (Eph. 4.1–6)

Even though he was speaking to a local city-wide church in Ephesus (which had its own cultural diversity), Paul's words are relevant to us today. His choice of words implies that he understands that what he is asking the Ephesians to do is not easy. It will take lowliness, gentleness, long-suffering, forbearing with one another, as they endeavour to keep the unity. For us today, unity in diversity is still critical. Jesus prayed for our unity when he was in Gethsemane:

> I ask not only on behalf of these, but also on behalf of those who will believe in me through their word, that they may all be one. As you, Father, are in me and I am in you, may they also be in us, so that the world may believe that you have sent me. The glory that you have given me I have given them, so that they may be one, as we are one, I in them and you in me, that they may become completely one, so that the world may know that you have sent me and have loved them even as you have loved me. (John 17.20–23)

The plea for unity anticipates that we will meet people who are different from us. Unity demands the presence of a different other. It requires difference and the possibility, or even likelihood, of disagreement and disunity. Yet, Jesus prays that we will be united. The psalmist is even more forceful in his language:

> How very good and pleasant it is
>   when kindred live together in unity!
> It is like the precious oil on the head,
>   running down upon the beard,
> on the beard of Aaron,
>   running down over the collar of his robes.

It is like the dew of Hermon,
   which falls on the mountains of Zion.
For there the LORD ordained his blessing,
   life for evermore. (Ps. 133)

Our unity is never just a matter of Christians getting along, although there
is that – those who want to have friends must themselves be friendly. But
it is both an act of obedience to Christ who said, 'it is by your love one for
another that the world will know that you are my disciples,' and a source
of spiritual power. When we are united, God blesses us with spiritual
authority. My grandmother used to remind us, her grandchildren, that
'our Christian unity breaks the back of the enemy'. She was right: unity
is strength. Even in the spiritual realm, we achieve more when we are
united. One can chase a thousand and two can put ten thousand to flight
(Deut. 32.30). God models diversity for us by being a Trinity. The three
Persons that make the Godhead can only function as a community. The
Father, the Son and the Spirit live together in a community of love where
absolute unity is normal, but it does not annul diversity. Paul may have
had this in mind when he wrote that 'we, who are many, are one body
in Christ, and individually we are members one of another' (Rom. 12.5)
and all are 'baptized by one Spirit so as to form one body' (1 Cor. 12.13).

Diversity and unity in the Spirit

The Church's very existence needs diversity. For it to exist as a global
fellowship of disciples of Christ – gathered and baptized into his one
body by his Spirit – there must be diversity, whether we are talking about
one congregation or the universal body of Christ. God designed the body
for diversity. It takes more than one to be Church. God is often revealed
in the presence of a different or irreducible other. Jesus said, 'where two
or three are gathered in my name, I am there among them' (Matt. 18.20).
Of course, one organ or member of the body cannot make the body. It
needs to belong with other members, different from itself, for it to be
alive and the body to be what it is meant to be – no member can survive
without the body, and the body cannot be alive and functional without
its members. In order for the body to be what it is meant to be and to
do what it is meant to do, it needs its members to contribute and play
their roles. Every member has a need that can only be met by other members. And by 'every member' I mean individual Christians, congregations,
and the regional or denominational churches to which they belong. No
member is self-sufficient; not one congregation or denomination on earth

has everything it needs within its own membership. Even affluent congregations that raise more money than they need will still lack something that can be met only by looking outside their own fellowship. Whether we like it or not, by God's design we need one another. Diversity is good both for our individual fellowships and for the entire body of Christ. Diversity within the body is required, and where diversity is lacking our understanding of both God and the Church is always limited.

This is the mission of the Spirit – to unite us so that we can be edified by the diversity of the body while at the same time enhancing our diversity so that we can be more united. This work of the Spirit is a continuation (and widening) of the mission of Jesus among the disciples. For those few years of ministry in Israel, and in addition to training them for ministry, Jesus sought to get the twelve disciples to become a team of friends, united in the Spirit, walking in one accord, and ready to face the world that would often seek to destroy them. The cross was, of course, important and the mission of the crucified God ought to remain central to our understanding of the ministry of Jesus. However, for the crucifixion to have worldwide implications, there was a need for a community of disciples to continue the work of witnessing for Christ after he had returned to heaven, carrying the uttermost parts of the earth and until the end of the age. If Jesus' mission to save the world was to actually happen, he had to form a body of united followers who would be empowered by the Spirit to be his witnesses in the face of persecution and martyrdom. He needed the tax collector, the Zealot and the fishermen to become one unit, kept together by the sense of mission that he gave them. Thus, the fellowship of the disciples would be the first domino of the chain of events that would 'turn the world upside down' (Acts 17.6). Their success in this mission would depend ultimately on their unity. Towards the end of their time together, Jesus gave them a new commandment: to 'love one another' (John 13.34–35). Unity would be that love in action, the outward expression of their love for one another. More important, it would give their evangelistic efforts the power they needed. Their love for one another – and the subsequent unity – would show the world that they are followers of Christ. When we get to the end of the Gospels (especially the final chapter of John) and the beginning of Acts, we notice that by the time Jesus left them to ascend to heaven they had become an inseparable group. When it looked like the mission had failed, and Peter decided to go back to Galilee to pick up fishing again (John 20), the others followed him. Jesus met them in Galilee, restored Peter, and sent them all back to Jerusalem – and again, they all returned. Nothing could separate them. When they came to Jerusalem, together, they prayed for a replacement for Judas so they could be twelve again

Is love enough?
w/ two diff. people

(Acts 1). They chose Matthias who, Luke points out, had been with them from the beginning (the baptism of John) to the day when Jesus was taken up (1.21–22). After three and a half years of working together, the twelve had become a united core among some 120 disciples, men and women from across the country, who would wait in prayer in the Upper Room.

Looking further, both in the Gospels and in Acts, it becomes rather evident that unity would be critical to their mission. They needed to become a united community that could weather the storms of opposition and persecution that were coming their way, starting with Jesus' humiliating public execution. It was embarrassing enough that their rabbi had been crucified. The fact that their rabbi claimed to be the Messiah – and they actually believed him, even though they did not understand what he meant – made it even more shameful. They would be forced to stay in hiding until the day of Pentecost, when emboldened by the Spirit they came out singing; 'let the entire house of Israel know with certainty that God has made him both Lord and Messiah, this Jesus whom you crucified' (Acts 2.36). Peter's sermon was effective on the day, but persecution was yet to come. Not long after, the disciples found themselves having to answer before the religious leaders. Some of their leaders would be imprisoned or killed. Many of them would be forced to flee from Jerusalem to find refuge around the Mediterranean world. It is only the Spirit who could keep them united and going.

Mission

As regards mission, multicultural congregations embody the theological justifications discussed above. The otherness of other cultures is not a threat, but a blessing for them to learn more about God and about themselves. The conviction of God's relational nature helps them relate with the other, even when there is no need to do so. As in the Ubuntu theology mentioned above, such congregations understand that the ministry of the stranger is needed for them to *be*.

They also embody the belief that the Spirit can use the other just as much as it uses them. Consequently they are not afraid of the other. They are eager to hear from them. The same is important when we talk about cross-cultural mission. There has recently been a move back to seeing Christ, and the Spirit, preceding the missionary into the mission field. This conversation has strengthened the argument that since the witness of the Spirit is found in every culture, it follows that every culture has some dignity within it. This is not the view that prevailed in missions in the past. When the missionaries came to Africa, it was common for them to condemn everything traditionally African as animistic or syncretistic. Africans were forced to abandon their cultures in order to adopt the superior culture of the missionary.

The incarnation holds a different model for us. It embodies an act of divine identification with the entire human race. Jesus Christ became a human person. It was an act of great humility and also of great respect to the human world. There is no condemnation of the human world. Human culture is dignified. Michael Frost and Alan Hirsch suggest that the incarnation provides a means by which the gospel can become a genuine part of a people group without damaging the innate cultural frameworks that provide the culture with a sense of meaning and history.[13] For multicultural contexts, the incarnation will require multicultural congregations.

Multicultural beginnings of the Church

In Acts 2, Luke brings us to Jerusalem on a day when the Shavuot (Feast of Pentecost) was taking place. The chapter begins with the 120 disciples 'all together in one place' (v.1) and then paints a picture of a gathering of many strangers in Jerusalem from 'every nation under heaven' (v.5), as far as the world was known at the time. Thus, before the thunderous outpouring of the Spirit and the tongues of fire, we see the seedlings of a multicultural community of followers of Jesus of Nazareth – diverse yet united. The disciples had been together as a group of men and women from both Palestine and the diaspora (from Capernaum on the northern shores of the Sea of Galilee as well as Cyrene in Libya and other parts of the Mediterranean world), spending more than seven days in the Upper Room, fasting and praying, hiding from the religious leaders in the city while waiting for the promise of the Spirit. That promise would be given on this particular day when Jerusalem was overflowing with visitors from around the world, when many Jews, proselytes and God-fearers were in Jerusalem to celebrate the festival. Luke goes on to list 15 nations present in Jerusalem, but it is likely that this list is by no means exhaustive, and many other nationalities may have been present. During festivals like Pentecost, Jerusalem was like the world in miniature. That is why Luke believes that there were Jews from *every nation under heaven*. Peter's sermon, citing Joel 2.28, promises the work of the Spirit upon all flesh – all people of the world (and not just the Jews). The 3,000 people from various parts of the world who would be added to the Church on that day represented the universal fellowship that was to come. Their conversion to the fellowship of the Nazarene was both a preview of and a down payment for the worldwide body of believers that we see today.

It was a day filled with miracles. Peter's use of Joel 2.28 to connect what was happening to the Old Testament is one of those miracles. It is impossible to tell from the Scriptures whether the disciples knew exactly what they were waiting for and how it would appear. Did they even know when it would come? They waited for ten days, until Pentecost Sunday, but Jesus had not indicated that the Spirit would fall on that specific day. His instruction was simply for them to 'wait in Jerusalem'. Both the disciples and the many people in the city seem to have been caught unawares. It was very early in the morning. The disciples were speaking in foreign languages that could be understood by the masses in Jerusalem on that day. Yet Peter understood what was happening: this event of the mighty rushing wind and the tongues of fire (plus the disciples speaking in tongues) was 'that which was spoken by the prophet Joel'. The promise of old was now being fulfilled, and all flesh, figuratively speaking, was in Jerusalem that day.

Then there is the triple-edged miracle of tongues. First, tongues of fire came from heaven and settled on the disciples. This was an unprecedented gesture. Fire had come down from heaven before to consume sacrifices (the tabernacle and 1 Kings 18) and as a chariot to take Elijah home (2 Kings 2). This time it was different. Even Joel (who is later invoked to explain the entire Pentecost event to the crowds) does not promise this. Most likely, Luke is trying to remind us of John the Baptist's prophecy that Jesus shall baptize with the Holy Ghost and with fire (Luke 3.16). During Jesus' baptism, the Spirit came down from heaven like a dove to settle upon Jesus. Pentecost would reflect the baptism of Jesus and would also fulfil John's promise – the disciples were baptized in the Spirit and fire. This event of the Spirit settling upon Jesus during his baptism, like the tongues of fire of Acts, has worldwide implications. In the baptism of Jesus, he was empowered to begin his ministry, which even though limited to the lost sheep of Israel was actually to save the entire world. John understood this when he declared, 'behold the Lamb of God that takes away the sin [not just of Israel but] of the world'. The tongues of fire symbolized the disciples being endued with power from on high to serve Christ not only in Jerusalem but in the entire world (Luke 24.49). This power would enable them to be Jesus' 'witnesses in Jerusalem, in all Judea and Samaria, and to the ends of the earth' (Acts 1.8).

Second, Luke makes a big deal of the disciples' ability to speak in tongues. The Spirit with which they were baptized gave the disciples utterance to speak in languages they did not know. It appears that they spoke in a mixture of *xenolalia* (foreign languages spoken by people in other parts of the world that could be heard and understood by those present in Jerusalem that morning) and *glossolalia* (spiritual languages that make no sense to the human mind). This act of speaking in tongues democratized their worship. They could all worship in the same 'language' regardless of their cultural background. Speaking in tongues gave them a new means of communication – a language and platform that would enable a diverse community to worship together across dividing lines. The tongues were a symbolic promise that the scattered nations (that came into being in Genesis 11 when God dispersed humanity for wanting to build a tower that could reach the heavens) could speak one spiritual language to God and to one another.

Third, we note the miracle of people's ability to understand the disciples' *xenolalia*. The people who had travelled to Jerusalem from the wider world heard the disciples worshipping God in their home languages – and were amazed. Jews from Carthage heard the disciples worship in Carthaginian. Parthians, Medians and Cappadocians heard the disciples in their own languages. This is the initial impact of Pentecost. The Spirit begins to connect with the nations – and it does this not by making them speak one language but by allowing them to hear the gospel in their own language. God was quite intent on reaching the nations. The pouring out of the Spirit happened on the day of the feast of Pentecost so that the nations that had gathered in Jerusalem could begin to hear the good news and – of course – witness the beginnings of the movement set to turn the entire world upside down. Despite its humble beginnings as a small community around the unlikely Messiah from Nazareth, this movement would have worldwide implications. Its inception in Acts 2 thrusts it onto the world stage because it was primarily brought into existence to reach the world. Jerusalem was just the first stop on a long journey that 2,000 years later has reached all nations. The first post-Pentecost community in Jerusalem, diverse as they were, would form a fellowship that

> devoted themselves to the apostles' teaching and fellowship, to the breaking of bread and the prayers. Awe came upon everyone, because many wonders and signs were being done by the apostles. All who believed were together and had all things in common; they would sell their possessions and goods and distribute the proceeds to all, as any had need. Day by day, as they spent much time together in the temple, they broke bread at home and ate their food with glad and generous hearts, praising God and having the goodwill of all the people. (Acts 2.42–47).

The Spirit had to be poured out on a day when the world was in Jerusalem. As the people returned to their home cities they would take with them the initial witness of the strange event that occurred during the Shavuot, of how they heard men and women declare great things about God in their own languages at nine in the morning, and how a Galilean man preached a sermon about Jesus of Nazareth that led to the formation of a new religious movement. They would be the first international witnesses. Their testimony would prepare the way for those who would come later, when persecution arose in Jerusalem. As they scattered, the community would be extended to include Gentiles. Further diversity was the natural outcome, and with it came new questions to consider: how were they to speak of Jesus of Nazareth, a Jewish Messiah, to a Greek audience? How would they deal with this diversity? What about the Gentile Christians – did they need to become Jews to become Christians? Would they need to be circumcised in order to belong? A council was held (Acts 15) in which it was decided that Gentile Christians would stay Gentile. Diversity was given a certificate of approval – the Church would henceforth be a multicultural community. Jesus would acquire Gentile titles. The Jewish Messiah would be worshipped as *Christos* and *Kurios* by the Greeks and the Romans.

From Galilee to Jerusalem and beyond

During the time Jesus spent with the disciples, he slowly moved the locus of the ministry to Jerusalem, where the Galileans would meet Cyrenians, Alexandrians, Cypriots, Romans, and many others who would begin to take the message to the ends of the earth. It would have been difficult to reach the world from Capernaum. Jerusalem was ideal, especially as Jews from around the world would visit the city for festivals. God's agenda was much bigger than Palestine, and it would take the diaspora Jews to spread the gospel beyond Jerusalem, Judea and Samaria. It was necessary for Peter, James and John to connect with Barnabas, Paul and Timothy. Jerusalem was the place for this to happen. By the time we get to Acts 6, diaspora Jews are rising up – out of necessity – to take leadership positions. Seven of them are chosen to become deacons to help the mostly Galilean apostles in taking care of the new community. When one of them is killed in Acts 7, further persecution begins to scatter the wider community. Both diaspora and Palestinian Jews were forced to leave Jerusalem, which of course created a new Christian diaspora. While the Palestinian Jews did not want to evangelize Gentiles, the diaspora Jews of Cyprus made a commitment to preach to Gentiles, and before long

a church was born in Antioch (Acts 11). A little while later, the Holy
Spirit shows up at one of their meetings and sends Barnabas and Saul on
a mission trip to evangelize some cities in Asia Minor. Thus, the gospel
was slowly going out from Jerusalem and in the process a faith community that included different nations, tribes and tongues was coming
into existence.

The Spirit brings diversity

As followers of Christ and members of the wonderful fellowship of the
Spirit, God calls us to live out (and possibly to enjoy and celebrate) our
diversity in unity. The Spirit of God does not seek to erase our diversity or expunge our differences. God calls us to worship in our various
languages and cultural traditions while being in unity with others who
worship in languages and cultures different from our own. The Spirit
gives diverse gifts to various members of the body, both in any local
congregation and in the universal communion of believers. Understood
this way, we see that the Spirit of God is the author of diversity in the
body of Christ. The Spirit of God shapes, gifts and tasks us differently,
and all this – being entirely God's own business – is dependent upon only
what God wants to give the body through us. Paul puts it well: 'There are
varieties of gifts, but the same Spirit; and there are varieties of services,
but the same Lord; and there are varieties of activities, but it is the same
God' (1 Cor. 12.4). Diversity within the body of Christ is not the enemy,
nor is it a work of the enemy. In local congregations or within wider
Christian communities, diversity is never to be thought of as a problem.
Christian diversity is always a blessing. Difference ought not to be feared.
God gives us gifts in the form of the different other who comes bearing
some of what we need to thrive. It is God who brings us together. Diversity is God's gift to us. What matters is what we do next. Speaking to the
worldwide body of Christians we could ask: now that we have found
diversity, what shall we do with it? This same question could be asked of
my friends in London: what shall we do with the fact that we are the most
diverse Church in one city in the whole world?

We can respond to diversity in various ways. We can refuse it, close
our borders, tell Christians from other nations they are not welcome here,
deporting those who are already here. We can make sure that people who
are different from us do not present themselves to us or affect our communities. Or we can choose to ignore diversity altogether and continue
to live as if the strangers among us do not exist. We may work with them
during the week, or meet them at the school gates as we send our children

to the same schools, but we can continue to ignore their faith and make sure that they do not come to our churches on Sunday or, if they do, we do all the talking and their role is to listen to us. Or, as often happens, they can rent our church hall or sanctuary for their own worship. Naturally, this rejection will force the strangers to form their own communities in which they can attempt to enjoy whatever dignity they can maintain in a strange land where they are invisible. Or, as is the hope of the argument of this book, we can embrace diversity and edify one another through the exchange of the gifts that God has given us for one another.

As long as we follow the one Spirit of God, our diversity will be used by God to reveal Godself to us all. God brings us together so that we can receive from one another the gifts that God gives to us through our neighbours. Our diversity is a gift from God – a precious gift that is too valuable to waste. It is to be sought after, not shunned. It is what makes us the body. It teaches us generosity, vulnerability and hospitality – three very critical postures in the Christian walk. In generosity, God gives us gifts to pass along and bless others, so we learn to discern and share with whoever among us needs the gifts that we bear. In vulnerability we have to open our hands to receive, for one cannot receive anything with a closed hand. We need to extend an open hand in order to receive something, and this gesture, especially towards a stranger, renders us vulnerable. It shows that there is nothing hidden in one's hand as much as it shows that one is expecting to receive. For us in the West it is always easier to give than to receive, and most of the time when we give it is in a non-relational way. Being in the body means that we must relate and share.

The *ekklesia* of Christ needs to figure out how to stay united in diversity if it is to hold together. It cannot survive if groups of Christians isolate themselves from fellowship with other Christians. It would change our theology – our ecclesiology – if we behaved as if we believe that we need one another in order to survive. Our congregations would act differently if they felt that they needed the congregation around the corner from them in order to thrive. The Nigerian congregation at one end of the street needs the Anglican congregation at the other. Similarly, the Australian church plant needs the Ghanaian church that it is trying to push out of business in its neighbourhood. Paul is helpful again here. 'If one member suffers, all suffer together with it; if one member is honoured, all rejoice together' (1 Cor. 12.26). He is effectively calling us to identify with the shortcomings of one another.

Notes

1 Aylward Shorter, *Toward a Theology of Inculturation* (Maryknoll, NY: Orbis, 1989), p. 29.

2 John Zizioulas, *Communion and Otherness: Further Studies in Personhood and the Church* (New York: T & T Clark, 2006), pp. 4–5 (my emphasis).

3 Zizioulas, *Communion and Otherness*, p. 5.

4 Zizioulas, *Communion and Otherness*, p. 6.

5 John 12.23.

6 Michael Welker, *God the Spirit* (Minneapolis, MN: Fortress Press, 1994), p. 232.

7 Welker, *God the Spirit*, p. 233.

8 See Miroslav Volf, *Exclusion and Embrace: A Theological Exploration of Identity, Otherness, and Reconciliation* (Nashville, TN: Abingdon Press, 1996), p. 51. Christians can depart without leaving, and therefore maintain distance but at the same time continue belonging.

9 Volf, *Exclusion and Embrace*, p. 48.

10 See Craig A. Carter, *Rethinking Christ and Culture: A Post-Christendom Perspective* (Grand Rapids, MI: Brazos Press, 2006).

11 Volf, *Exclusion and Embrace*, p. 49.

12 Volf, *Exclusion and Embrace*, p. 52.

13 Michael Frost and Alan Hirsch, *The Shaping of Things to Come: Innovation and Mission for the 21st-Century Church* (Peabody, MA: Hendrickson, 2003), p. 37.

8

Multicultural Ecclesiology

The Christian Church, as I have argued so far, has great potential to bring people of different cultures, races and social standing together in worship communities. This is what following Christ really means – that there will be neither Jew nor Greek in the global fellowship of disciples. When Christ does not bring us together, when multicultural fellowship is impossible, it is usually a sign that there is something wrong on our side. The Spirit of Jesus unites us together in diversity. The very name, *Christian*, should always remind us of the first multicultural community that worshipped together in Antioch in the 40s CE, standing out against other worshipping communities, and warranting the coining of a new word – *christianoi*. More often than not, as Christians, it is not the issue of belief that separates us. Our faith in Christ should unite us. The fellowship of the Spirit of God makes unity possible in ways otherwise impossible. Following Christ, we will generally have the same core beliefs, at the centre of which is that Jesus, the Christ, the Son of God who became a Jewish man, lived in Palestine and died at Golgotha to save humankind from the destruction that comes because of humanity's sins. However, we interpret and manifest our beliefs in various ways, and rightly so. Everything we do as Christians is shaped by our culture and myriad other variables that make us live our faith in different ways. Though we may not admit it, our theologies, ecclesiologies and even missiologies are all shaped to a large extent by our circumstances. It has been said countless times, especially in academic theological and missiological discourse, that all theologies are contextual. I wish it was possible for us to actually behave as if we understood this to be true, and stop expecting European theologians to speak to the universal Church as if what they say is relevant in all parts of the world. There is no theology that is culture-free, but we still expect Karl Barth to speak relevantly to the Zulus of South Africa, the Navajos of the United States as well as the Koori of Australia. This is not possible, it does not make sense, and it is not necessary. Our understanding of God is shaped by how our culture perceives and talks about God. In addition, our ecclesiologies are shaped by the culture in which we are located. The way we understand church – how the Christian Church is supposed to be, how Christians are supposed to behave both when they congregate and when they are scattered in their neighbourhoods, what their churches are expected to do in society – is all shaped to a large extent by our cultures. Good ecclesiological discourse will recognize that every expression of church reflects the culture in which it emerged. It anticipates that there will be differences in the expressions of church from one culture to another. This is to be expected – and in most cases encouraged.

The argument for multicultural ecclesiology being made in this book is founded upon two convictions. First, as discussed earlier, cultural diversity is fast becoming the new normal in British society, as witnessed by the national census. Britain gets a bit more colour every year both through migration and also through BAME people already here giving birth to non-white or mixed-race children. British does not necessarily mean white any more. The impact of diversity on British culture is becoming ever more noticeable in various aspects of the British life. An obvious example of this is how, in popular television culture, viewers now expect to see diversity in the programmes they watch, no matter what channel airs them. Most TV dramas now include not just racial diversity but a mixture in genders, sexual orientation and ages among their cast. On more than one occasion viewers have demanded more diversity: in the US version of the TV series *The Bachelor* (produced by ABC), for example, a handsome male courts a group of equally good-looking females in order to find *the one*, and it has been recently questioned why the bachelors in all 23 seasons of the show so far have been white. Similarly, in 2015, the hashtag #oscarsowhite went viral on the subject of the mainly white Oscar nominations line-up, in spite of the many non-white actors featuring in successful movies that year. In addition, in 2018, the British public got into a rather heated debate around the question of the race (and even gender) of the celebrated film character James Bond, who has been played by five British, one Australian and one Irish white male actors. The rumour was that the next James Bond could be Idris Elba, a black actor of Sierra Leonean and Ghanaian parents. While many could not stomach the idea of a black James Bond, such a discourse would have been impossible ten years ago – so at least we are talking about it. Is it finally possible to have a black Bond? An all-white *EastEnders* would certainly raise a few eyebrows. When even the general populace expects and demands diversity on the social arena, we cannot justify all-white or all-black congregations. In the current social milieu of Britain, it should be impossible for the Church to justify segregation.

Second, and as a result of the reasons given above, congregations that exist in places of cultural diversity will do well to reflect the diversity in their membership. I understand that this is not an easy task. Pastors often ask me, 'Why are you asking us to do this difficult work, which does not even bring back much reward?' Yet, I still believe that multiculturalism enriches the Church much more than it demands us to give of ourselves. The very process of figuring out how to worship with a different other is what makes the Church what it is. One African woman, after hearing me plead with the leadership of her congregation to consider being a little more welcoming to African asylum seekers, some of whom had been sent by the government to her parish, told a story of the pain she had endured when she was new in her congregation and she had had to carry the food she had contributed back home from church because nobody had touched it (either not knowing the food or not trusting her cooking). Her vicar responded by highlighting his own helplessness as he could not communicate well with her because of her lack of fluency in English. But together, in their openness and vulnerability, they found a way to communicate. The vicar encouraged the congregation to at least try her food, making a point about how much he loved her samosas and *mandasi*. Now, many years later, there is never an event at church when her food is not made available; the congregation often asks her to cater for other events, even those taking place outside the church.

If we don't have to deal with others different from us, we can easily forget how to be vulnerable with one another. We are not at the centre of the universe, therefore we need others to remind us that the centre is out there – in God. Such a disposition requires humility on our part. The need to see, recognize, acknowledge, listen to, learn from, and adapt ourselves to be hospitable to people of different cultures reminds us of such vulnerability and, if we persist, it helps us understand God better. Through the eyes of the other we are able to see God in a different light, which always enriches our understanding of God even if we don't agree with what we see.

Our ecclesiologies are significantly shaped by culture. This is something that congregational leaders need to wrestle with at all times, asking themselves, 'What is our culture?' There are two sides to this question. In the first place, congregations need to understand what culture shapes them. Second, they have to be aware of the culture they live out together as a community as well as portray to those outside the congregation. They need to address various questions: Who are we? What culture shapes us? Why do we do what we do? And why do we do it the way we do it? On the British Christian landscape, a majority of the congregations will do well to notice that their ecclesiology is shaped more by general Western middle-class values than the gospel itself. A great deal of our understanding of community and belonging reflects the Western marks of individualism and capitalism. That is why most British denominations – including the

Church of England – find it hard to connect with lower-class parts of the society. I suspect that an ecclesiology for economically depressed areas might involve a different dress code from that seen in most congregations around the country. I would also anticipate a different type of language, different musical tastes, and sometimes a flexibility around the times of church services, among other aspects of our ecclesiology.

African churches in Britain are also divided, quite strictly, along tribal and national lines. It is common knowledge that the Redeemed Christian Church of God (RCCG) is a Nigerian denomination. More than 90 per cent of their membership in the United Kingdom is Nigerian. However, this is only a half-truth. It is Yoruba. They must be commended for their hard work attempting to adapt their ecclesiology to Britain – it is impossible to find a Yoruba-speaking RCCG congregation in the United Kingdom. Yet, aspects of Yoruba culture are evident in how they do church, especially in the way they use and wield power. Similarly, the Church of Pentecost (CoP) from Ghana has more than 95 per cent of their members identify as Ghanaian (or originally from Ghana, as many love to say). However, it is mostly Ghanaians of the Akan community that make up the membership both in the United Kingdom and in Ghana. Their ecclesiology seems (to other Ghanaians) to have simply Christian-ized and baptized Akan culture. Everything, from the way they sing and dance in their services to the organization of their leadership hierarchy, is a pure reflection of Akan tribal systems. Here in the United Kingdom, the Church of Pentecost has three times more Twi-speaking congregations than English-speaking ones.

These two denominations – the RCCG and the CoP, by far the largest African denominations in the United Kingdom, with well over a thousand congregations between them – can easily be identified by their national and tribal origins. The same can be said of many other smaller African denominations in the United Kingdom. The Apostolic Faith Mission is predominantly Zimbabwean and South African in its membership and it reflects some of the culture of these countries in the way it organizes itself. Both the Living Waters Church and the Calvary Family Church are Malawian and reflect Malawian cultures in everything they do. Across the United Kingdom, we find Congolese, Kenyan, Ugandan and Ethiopian churches that reflect well the cultures of their countries of origin. A Nigerian of Igbo heritage would realize upon entering a Yoruba church that she had crossed cultural boundaries. A Malawian entering a Zambian church will find that their 'this is the way we do things' is different from his Malawian congregation, even though the two countries are neighbours and share some of their ethnic communities and languages.

The case for multicultural churches

In my argument so far, I have highlighted the need for contextualization in both our theologies and ecclesiologies. Thus, our discourse on multicultural ecclesiology must start with acknowledging that different churches will be shaped by different cultures, and that they will express these cultures differently in their worship. Leaders will do well to understand that there is no such thing as a culture-free ecclesiology, and it is therefore helpful for churches to reflect critically on the cultures that shape them and that they exhibit in their worship. Unfortunately, the cultural embeddedness of our ecclesiologies means that there will always be some members who are 'inside' and others who are 'outside' the cultures that drive our congregations. A black person in a white congregation will generally be an outsider, and the same applies for a white person in a black congregation. But it is not just colour that separates insiders from outsiders. A Malawian in a Nigerian congregation may feel like an outsider just as much as a Mexican would in a Russian congregation. An Oromo Christian would be a stranger in an Amhara congregation even though both Oromo and Amharic people are Ethiopian. In order to avoid this type of awkwardness in either being cultural outsiders or insiders having to adapt their cultures to allow outsiders to belong, each group tends to form their own congregation, and so the practice continues that prefers insiders and marginalizes outsiders. The proposition being made here is that congregational life is more whole when in the context of cultural diversity it involves a multicultural community – when people of different cultures commit to worshipping together, each contributing aspects of their cultures to create a *culture of many cultures*. A truly multicultural congregation will have room for all the cultures within it to thrive, at the same time helping them realize that together they make what the Church is.

Culturally expanding congregations

Multicultural congregations learn to manage the tension between whatever culture they embrace as their own *congregational culture* on the one hand and the many subcultures of their members on the other. They have to make a commitment to not let go of either, needing to find a 'sweet spot' between 'only one culture matters' (which is usually said to be the *kingdom culture*, as if the kingdom of God has one culture for all human beings) and 'all cultures matter' (which often makes it difficult for cultures to engage with one another and to share). Letting go of their congregational culture would mean them turning into small communities of monocultural Christians with little possibility of sharing whatever gifts they have with others, while letting go of their members' cultural identities would mean assimilation, ignoring their cultural gifts, and in the process dehumanizing them. Great multicultural congregations realize that their congregational culture has to be the authentic aggregate of the cultures of their members. They have to develop and embrace a culture that makes space for a variety of subcultures to thrive together, that is expansive enough to welcome new subcultures into its mix, highlighting them and encouraging them to share their gifts with the wider congregation. When a new culture joins – or a new member from a culture so far unrepresented – everything about the congregation's culture changes. If a Nigerian family joins a white British congregation, that congregation cannot continue with business as usual. They have to reshape their culture in the light of the Nigerians among them – which means learning their Nigerian names, their greetings, about their food, and even incorporating a few Nigerian songs in their worship services. They might acquire a few Nigerian books for the church library, or maybe some drums for their music ministries. Above all, they have to encourage the Nigerian family to share whatever gifts they bring for the enrichment of the wider congregation. They would repeat the process for a family from Zimbabwe, the Philippines, or Brazil – at which point their worship songbook might expand considerably.

Models of multicultural congregations

Multicultural congregations, by definition, will include people of more than one culture in their membership and worship services. The degree to which the different cultures manifest and influence one another varies. In this book, 'multicultural churches' are understood to be different from 'multi-ethnic churches' even though these terms are often used interchangeably elsewhere. A multi-ethnic church comprises people of different ethnicities (which naturally includes races) but this does not guarantee a multiplicity of cultures. A congregation can have black and white people who may be racially different but share more cultural similarities than differences. In the northern parts of England, for example, black suburban college-educated and middle-class people are not too different from their white counterparts. They can belong to one congregation and have one culture in spite of their skin colour. It is also possible for a congregation of one race of people to have several cultures represented, but this is generally rare. My interest is in congregations that have different cultures worshipping together, and my argument stands even for those congregations of one race but many cultures.

Several models of multicultural congregations exist today. For this conversation, only three are helpful (partly because some congregations that say they are multicultural are not really multicultural), and are discussed below.

Monocultural congregations sharing multicultural worship

First, there are multicultural congregations that are made of several smaller monocultural fellowships that worship separately in their own communities but come together for multicultural worship every so often with other communities of different cultures. They usually have some form of covenant or relationship, especially among the leaders, that allows them to meet perhaps once a month for worship. The leaders know one another and try to help their congregations to know each other as well. Members generally follow along but are not ready to worship multiculturally on a weekly basis. This model generally serves as a taster for congregations exploring becoming a multicultural community. I know of a network of congregations in the Midlands that includes Zimbabwean, Zambian, South African and white British congregations. All these have their own services for three Sundays in a month, and they get together on the fourth Sunday for multicultural worship. In their own congregations, they embody their own cultures faithfully; for the Africans, they wear African dress, sing African songs, listen to African sermons (sometimes in African languages) and eat African food. On the Sundays when they meet with the other congregations, everyone speaks English. Only the white British congregation has a hall large enough to accommodate the entire network, so, all the joint meetings happen at their location, which often means that the British congregation tends to facilitate the services. For these services, each congregation is expected to let go of their culture and adopt a culture that all congregations can understand and relate to. Ironically, this translates to the white British congregation's culture. Of course, they call themselves a multicultural church, but very little multicultural worship seems to take place.

Monocultural fellowships in a multi-ethnic church

Larger denominational churches often have small groups of people of similar cultures among their membership. These minority cultures tend to need space to connect with each other and remind one another of their own identity. If they are immigrants – which is usually the case – there is often need for them to share aspects of life as they knew it at home. They love to get together to eat familiar food, hear news about what is happening back home, and catch up with old friends. Parents love to discuss how they are raising their children in a foreign culture. However, most importantly, many like to get together to worship in their mother tongue. Music and songs in their own language, which for many Africans form the liveliest part of a worship service, are a cultural phenomenon that brings back old memories, transports them back home, and makes their worship experience complete.

An example of this type of multicultural church is a Church of England congregation in the north of England that has Iranian and Zimbabwean minority fellowships within it. These Iranian and Zimbabwean Christians are part of the normal worship service every Sunday but are not represented in the higher levels of congregational leadership. The services are traditional Church of England – there is little room to adapt to the presence of the Iranians and Zimbabweans. Once in a while they may be invited to read the Scriptures or to lead intercessory prayers, but under normal circumstances it is rare to see them taking part in leading the worship service. To try to make them feel welcome, or to compensate for a general lack of diversity in the leadership, the minority groups are allowed to have their own fellowships once a month. An Iranian or a Zimbabwean priest comes from the Midlands to lead worship. At these services Iranian and Zimbabwean worship music can be heard, and it is not unusual for them to have their entire services in Farsi or Shona.

There is a large Catholic congregation in Glasgow that has more Polish and Congolese Christians than white British Christians. A Polish priest has been employed to officiate the Mass in Polish, and a Cameroonian priest leads the Mass in French for the Congolese members. On a weekly basis, though, the Mass is still in English. The Polish and Congolese members have their own minority fellowships that take place on alternate Sunday afternoons. Altogether, they form a multicultural congregation even though their diversity does not show in the leadership, and the Mass does not reflect the diversity seen in the congregation.

These two models are the most popular, and are what people often mean when they talk about multicultural churches. Congregations generally fall short of true multiculturalism in their worship. Minority cultures are tolerated by or subsumed (or assimilated) into the dominant majority culture of the congregation, but are then allowed to meet for their minority worship somewhere at the margins of the congregation's life. The congregation usually has limited access to the gifts of the minority culture. The Catholic congregation in Glasgow mentioned above is very Scottish in its culture. Both the Polish and the Congolese members are expected to fit in with the existing worship system, but are allowed to have their own occasional services on the side. The Church of England congregation does the same thing. Foreign Anglicans are welcome as long as they are happy to contribute a foreign song or dance every so often in addition to having their own service every month where they can worship in their mother tongue.

Multicultural churches

A fully multicultural congregation will be different, and this is what the third model is about. True multicultural congregations happen when all cultures – both host and guest – intentionally displace themselves from the centre to allow for the emergence of a new culture that comes out of all cultures present working together. In practice, they take turns serving God in the spotlight, each bringing the best of their culture to share with others. Consequently, all groups – majority and minority, local and foreign – become guests at the Lord's table where God becomes the host. Such congregations encourage all cultures to contribute to everything that is happening in the church. Each culture brings a gift and the congregation learns to receive from others while giving whatever they have to share. One group may be gifted in prayer, another in singing, another in hospitality; they together keep the congregation running. A worship service can represent several cultures – a psalm from one, a prayer from another, a sermon from maybe two cultures preaching together, songs from different cultures, often sung in their original languages and making use of different genres of music. This is what a multicultural ecclesiology will look like. A congregation might hold bilingual or multilingual services, such as in African congregations in Britain where the older generation needs to communicate in their languages or worship in their vernaculars while the younger generation is more fluent in English. The same approach can work where English people worship together with non-English speakers.

Often, this type of church is only possible when the leadership team itself is multicultural. The various cultural groups need to be represented in the decision-making systems of their congregations, and the people addressing the congregation, those holding the microphone or standing on the podium or in the pulpit, have to represent the cultural diversity of the congregation. Even more, congregations aspiring to become multicultural must embrace, empower and showcase the minority leaders already in their midst. Generally speaking, members of minority groups will feel more comfortable when they see people from their own cultures in front, leading some aspect of worship. Leaders have to model for their members how to value diversity. Authentic multicultural leaders are open to hear, to dialogue with, to learn from and to encourage people of different cultures. This is the catholic personality that realizes that while people are of one particular culture, the Holy Spirit has baptized them into the body of Christ that is made of people of many cultures, and none of the cultures is superior.

Forget how many nationalities attend your church

It has become fashionable nowadays to keep count of the nationalities that attend our congregations. I often hear pastors boast how many nationalities they have in their churches. They go on to list the nationalities one by one. Not wanting to be outdone, another pastor usually responds with a larger figure than the first one. Most of the time, this is said as a way of testifying to the goodness of God that has taken the ministry across the nations. However, it also generally serves to say, 'Our congregation is significant. Look how many people from other nations belong here.' It often seems like a competition among congregations – let us see who can have the most nationalities in one church.

When talking of the many nationalities in their congregations, most pastors are basically thinking of assimilation. In the larger frame of things, they are wanting to show how many people have assimilated into their culture. Leaders of multicultural congregations, however, hardly pay any attention to the nationalities of their members. Of course, they notice the nationalities, as they should, but they focus on the culture. They focus on shaping a congregation in which the many nationalities' cultures are expressed. Not every multinational church is multicultural. It is never about how many nationalities one can gather. Yes, there may be many nationalities in a congregation, but that means little if they are unable to make their cultural contribution.

Negotiating power in multicultural congregations

Central to this discussion of multicultural congregations is the issue of power, and how power gets to be shared between the host and the stranger; for church leaders, it is about how they respond to the Spirit's call to diversity and how it democratizes both power and the *charismata*.

In fact, where multiculturalism is criticized, it will be usually on the issue of power. For dominant cultures, the power that comes with being a host – the owner of both the land and the show – can either foster or stifle cultural diversity. In Isaiah's vision of the peaceful reign of Christ at the end of time, he describes a wolf and lamb eating grass together.

> The wolf shall live with the lamb, and the leopard shall lie down with the kid, and the calf and the young lion and the fatling together; and a little child shall lead them. (Isa. 11.6)

The wolf has to restrain itself to dwell with the lamb. Or, as my people in southern Malawi would say, the wolf had to be emasculated to be sat together with a lamb that would otherwise be its food. It had to let go of its predator instincts in order to share fellowship with the lamb; it had to lay down its power. This is always the case in multicultural congregations; the wolves who hold the power must choose not to eat the lambs but have fellowship with them instead.

Gerald Arbuckle, writing in the 1980s, asserted that if multiculturalism is to exist, three types of power must be exercised by dominant and migrant societies. The first is what he calls nutritive power. This is the type of power that gives people a chance to develop their own inner capacities without babysitting or patronizing them. The second is integrative power. It involves individuals or groups working together for the benefit of all. The third is relational power, which is the willingness of all involved to learn from one another.[1] However, Arbuckle emphasizes that multiculturalism requires power-sharing as a prerequisite. Without power-sharing, talk of multiculturalism is simply a political fad.[2] Mark DeYmaz is of the same mind. His book *Building a Healthy Multi-ethnic Church* is dedicated to the practices required for a multicultural congregation. While he offers many important ideas, one that I find outstanding is called 'embracing dependence'.[3] It means that congregations have to learn to be vulnerable, in the true sense of the word, to depend both on God and on the stranger for their being. This is radically different from how most congregations think. To embrace dependence, congregants have to let go of their powerful positions in order to be ministered to by the other. Jesus, in Luke 10, suggests that the disciples had to depend on the hospitality of the stranger. Jesus advises his disciples to go without carrying a purse or a spare sandal. They would have to depend on the hospitality of strangers. In John 13, Jesus washes the feet of the disciples. It is an embodiment of the self-emptying nature of Christ. True inclusion will always involve *kenosis*.

Notes

1 Gerald A. Arbuckle, *Earthing the Gospel: An Inculturation Handbook for Pastoral Workers* (Maryknoll, NY: Orbis, 1990), p. 182.

2 Arbuckle, *Earthing the Gospel*, p. 181.

3 Mark DeYmaz, *Building a Healthy Multi-ethnic Church: Mandate, Commitments, and Practices of a Diverse Congregation* (San Francisco, CA: Jossey-Bass, 2007).

9

One New Tribe

Humans are tribal beings. We are social animals that mix and mingle within our tribes. We make our tribes, and they make us. Without them, we often become miserable. In Malawi we teach children from a very young age about the importance of belonging: that *kalikokha nkanyama, tili tiwiri ntianthu*, literally translates as 'the one who is alone is an animal, and those who are a pair (or simply, those who are two) are human beings', while *chala chimodzi sichiswa nsabwe* means 'one thumb alone does not kill headlice' – a figurative way of saying 'one cannot solve all problems alone'. These are only two of many proverbs – I could easily list another ten – that are employed to teach young people that it is not human to live in isolation. They can only be human when in communion with other humans. Our understanding of life makes us believe that no one can really exist in isolation, and fundamentally a person is only a person if he or she belongs to a community (family, clan, village, tribe, etc.). Typical of cultures in the southern part of Africa, Malawians believe in the concept of *umunthu* (similar to *ubuntu* in South Africa), which says, 'I am because we are'. Essentially, we teach children to say, 'I belong, therefore I am'. It takes individuals to make a community, but it also takes a community to make the individuals. While individuality is appreciated, individualism is frowned upon – it weakens the tribe.

The folly of tribalism

For people all over the world, life without community is impossible. Isolation and exclusion, even as a form of punishment, are dehumanizing. It is, indeed, the folly of our Western mindsets that individualism is one of the primary lenses through which we look at life. We often aim to be self-sufficient and therefore to have no need to speak to our neighbours, especially if the neighbours look or speak differently from us. Our screens, both the small pocket-sized ones that accompany us every waking hour and the big ones that wait for us in our living rooms, tend to individualize us further. We rarely lift up our heads to see the strangers that surround us. Individualism has made us a generation of loners, trying to figure out life each one on our own. 'Each one for themselves and God for us all' has left us unable to socialize with our neighbours. Loneliness has become an epidemic. It is a serious public health concern which has become evident in young university students who find it difficult to make friends and cannot find someone to talk to when in need, and in older people who find it difficult to maintain relationships after retirement – and many other people in between. The social and financial cost of the individualization of Western societies will be higher than many can imagine. Depression and anxieties related to loneliness are the social disease of our generation. Books such as Robert Putnam's *Bowling Alone*[1] and Robert Bellah's *Habits of the Heart*[2] paint a heartbreaking image of what individualism can do to a society.

As humans we have a propensity to connect with others. It is natural for us to seek to relate to others, especially those who are familiar to us. We find our identities in our belongingness: to family, clan, tribe and nation, plus other communities such as the choir, the running club, the pub. Those who are familiar with us are usually those who are also similar to us. From early childhood we are all, in one way or another, socialized into our tribes – which means we begin to get a sense of who is in and who is out; who is like us and who is not. Of course, nobody tells the black kids – or the Asian kids – to sit together in the school cafeteria. It just happens. Our experience of the world and understanding of life are always mediated through the mind of the tribe. We are shaped by our tribes. From the family unit to our regional and national identities, humans are socialized to identify by their communities. These communities give us the languages that we use – distinct languages that mark us as different from the community in the next valley or the one from the other side of the globe.

In addition to being communal and tribal, we are also territorial. For centuries upon centuries, we – even the nomadic peoples of the savannah – lived in tribal lands. We are hardwired to belong, yet also to exclude those who do not belong with us from the commonwealth of our land and its resources. We belong in our families, our communities, our tribes and our nations, and we have a way of identifying those who belong with us and those who do not, who are then to be kept out. Paradoxically, while we are adamant about our individualism, we are also becoming more convinced about our national identities. The current political atmosphere in the West seems to be saying that the nation-states to which we belong should be recognized as independent and sovereign. Rising nationalisms in parts of Europe and North America reflect the individualization of the state. We project our individualism onto the nation-state, viewing them as sovereign and independent *individual* states. Ultimately the nation becomes our tribe and our individualized devotion to the state turns us into good patriotic citizens. We have thus returned to the territorial tribalism of old – only this form of tribalism is often hostile (usually passively but sometimes aggressively) not just to the immigrant stranger but to other tribes who have resources that we desire. It both thrives on and fuels a 'them-against-us' understanding of human society. Each tribe places itself at the centre of the human narrative, finding everyone else threatening and needing to protect their livelihood. Whether it is Brexit or 'America First', we are seeing a manifestation of this territorial tribalism, and it looks as if Western Christianity is complicit.

Western cultures on the surface seem to have done away with tribalism, yet they are just as tribalistic. They appear not to have the ethnic groups that we call 'tribes' elsewhere. When they talk about tribes, it generally has nothing to do with ethnic heritage – because, of course, the language of 'tribes' was pejoratively used during the colonial era to demean the 'uncivilized heathens'. Without the strong ethnic structures that hold people together between the family on the one hand and the nation-state on the other, people form tribal allegiances around other aspects of life, like sports, religion and professions. Ethnic tribal identities have been replaced by transient associations and fellowships built around concepts and ideologies that never really do what ethnic tribes are supposed to do for us. Beneath the national identity, there are still many tribal tendencies. For instance, saying 'I am English' is usually a sufficient identifier, even though hearers may perceive a Scouse or a Mancunian accent. To distinguish themselves properly, the same person could say, 'I am a Liverpudlian' or 'I am a Mancunian', and such a statement can have tribal connotations – a tribalism that comes on full display when football teams from Liverpool and Manchester play each other. Rivalry between football clubs and their cities (or cities and their football clubs) is distinctly tribal. On a wider European scale, saying 'I am English' also means 'I am not French or German', which is just as tribal. In addition, the class wars that exist between the poor and the affluent can also turn tribalistic. Some tribes are formed around professional associations, such as accountants or lawyers, and these also often behave like they are a tribe. In 'tribes', people have a sense of belonging to a group both for what they get out of the group and for what they bring to it. Many of these tribal identities are fluid – they change according to people's circumstances and commitments. While a Welsh person remains Welsh wherever she lives, and thus her national tribe stays the same, her professional tribe may change as she moves from one career to another. But, above all, the nation-state, with its territorial sovereignty, has become the super-tribe.

The Church and tribes

It is rather unfortunate that the Church of Christ often lends itself to cultural exclusivism and tribalism. The history of the Church is rather clear on this; the Christian life tends to follow – and therefore be shaped by – our tribal identities. The sad reality of the Rwandan genocide of 1994 (in which around a million Christians were killed by other Christians for being of a different tribe) showed the world that tribal allegiance is more powerful than Christianity. The blood of ethnicity was said to be stronger than the water of baptism. Here in Europe, in the two great wars of the twentieth century Christian nation-states fought other Christian nation-states in spite of sharing the same faith. This continues in many aspects of our lives; we tend to put our tribal identity above our faith.

Christ seeks to engage with nations, tribes and tongues at their core, and this is usually at the centre of their cultural selves. Just as a culture-free theology does not exist, there is also no such thing as a culture-free ecclesiology. For Christianity to take root among a people, it must engage the people's culture and they – the people – must find ways for Christ to be comprehensible in their language and worldview. There is also no culture-free congregation. Each congregation is uniquely shaped by culture, and every congregation manifests its cultural commitments. From the music they sing to the make-up of their leadership teams and the activities they run, it is usually easy to discern the culture that shapes them (and consequently who is welcome and who is not among them). Consequently, it is rather easy for congregations and denominations to become tribalistic. This is extremely common among African Christians, but it is also clearly visible among Westerners. My work in North America has brought me into contact with German Lutherans in Saint Paul and Swedish Lutherans in Minneapolis, as well as, in London, the Akan-dominated Church of Pentecost from Ghana and the Yoruba-majority Redeemed Christian Church of God from Nigeria. I have seen some congregations who believe that God has called them to be of one specific tribe *and no other*. A pastor I met in London recently assured me that God sent him to London to evangelize only Yorubas. Within Africa, a great deal of this comes from the work of the missionaries who often divided their work according to tribes. The Anglicans, Methodists, Presbyterians and even Catholics would focus their work on particular tribes to the point that in some countries it is possible to identify tribes by their denominations.

Christianity's relationship with the tribes needs careful reflection. God's own work with the nation of Israel, which is reflected in Jesus' work with the twelve disciples, is rooted in the tribes. John's visions in the book of Revelation suggest a possibility that there will be tribes in heaven. He describes people from every tribe and tongue worshipping before the throne. It is possible that he comes to this conclusion because the multitude that he sees can only be real if it includes people from all the tribes in the world, but it is also possible that he could identify the many different tribes, enough to conclude that all tribes in the world were represented. If the latter is correct, it means that we will bring our tribal identities to heaven. There will be heavenly tongues – whatever they will sound like – but our tribal languages will also be spoken. There will be chiChewa, Ojibwe and French spoken there. Being a culturally shaped and locally situated Christian, as we all are, should cause us to figure out how to be a faithful follower of Christ in our particular corner of the world as well as in the universal body of Christ. We are always missional bridges between our communities and cultures and the wider communion of believers around the world. The old question of whether one can be an African and a Christian at the same time becomes critical again. Conversion to Christianity does not mean that we have to adopt a foreign culture. Scholars such as Andrew Walls and Lamin Sanneh have told us over the decades that the gospel is both a prisoner and liberator of cultures. So, the gospel makes us seek to embody the godly best of our tribes but does that to help us contribute, from our tribes' resources, to the global body of Christ.

Christianity is translatable enough to withstand being infinitely embedded in the cultures of each of the world's tribes. In fact, Christianity is most authentic and powerful when it is completely contextualized – when it looks and speaks local. Translation, in this conversation, means much more than making the Bible and the hymns available in local languages. That is important, but it is usually just the first step in contextualizing Christianity. For Christianity to be effectively contextualized, everything must be translated – the practices, the services, the mediums of worship. World Christianity can only be world Christianity if it is contextualized. In Acts, the contextualization of the gospel is embodied in the translation of the name and title of Christ himself. Jews would recognize the name 'Yeshuah' and understand the concept of a messiah – the long-awaited liberator who would set them free from Roman oppression. However, Yeshuah the *mashiach* (messiah) made little sense to the Greeks who were indifferent to the Jewish political scene. When the story of Jesus was told among the Gentiles, the very name Yeshua was translated Iesous, *mashiach* became *Christos* (Christ), and a new title, the *kurios* (lord or master), was employed (1 Cor. 12.3; Rom. 1.3–4; 10.9–13; Phil. 2.11). This the Greeks would understand with no problem.

Indeed, there should not be one expression of Christianity that is exported and replicated in other parts of the world. To the dismay of many of my European Reformed friends and missionaries, John Calvin will not speak to twenty-first-century Malawian Presbyterians like he did to the nineteenth-century Church of Scotland that sent missionaries to Malawi, let alone to sixteenth-century Christians in Geneva who shaped a great deal of Calvin's theology. Lutheranism in Germany has to look and behave differently from Lutheranism in Kenya. Even the best of contemporary Western theologians and Christian leaders need to be understood in context; they need to be contextualized if they are to speak to a wider global audience. The Anglican Church in Britain (or the Church of England, as it is properly called) has to be different from the Anglican Church in Nigeria or the Anglican Church in Uganda, because in those African countries the gospel can only take root if it is translated. Unfortunately, this is usually not the case. The Anglican Church of Malawi, for instance, is often said to be more conservative and even more 'high church' than the Church of England as it currently stands, as well as the USPG missionaries who established it. Similarly, the Redeemed Christian Church of God (RCCG) in Lagos has to be different from its branches in London and Paris, just like the Church of Pentecost (CoP) in Accra has to be different from their congregations in Italy. The RCCG and CoP churches in Europe must translate themselves to speak to Europeans in ways that the Europeans can understand. Again, this is not what is happening. Many African churches in the diaspora find con-textualization to be an impossible task that brings little rewards, and they are thus out of context both wherever they are in the diaspora and back home where they came from (because they are not part of the continuing contextualization of their home church).

The clash of Christianities

The infinite translatability of the Church, or of Christianity in general, means that the faith will be expressed in a multitude of ways around the world. Each one of those expressions will be shaped by its context as it responds to the issues that the people concerned are wrestling with. In addition, each of those expressions will be to varying degrees different from all the others. As long as those expressions of Christianity remain in their own parts of the world, everything seems fine. South African Pentecostals do not have to worry about American Methodism until they find themselves evangelizing the same people in South Sudan. The differences do not really matter when they are invisible for lack of contact. It is when the different expressions of Christianity begin to encounter each other that we can see a clash. When Christians from one part of the world come into contact with Christians from another part of the world, the differences begin to stand out. British Anglicans do not need to worry about what Nigerian Pentecostals believe until the latter show up in Britain and begin to influence the religious landscape. Of course, the story of contemporary Western Christianity is shaped by these encounters of Christianities from various parts of the world. The religious landscape of contemporary Europe and North America shows a growing presence of African, Asian and Latin American Christianities. We could, for instance, talk of the many Filipino congregations in Italy or Spain, or the number of Ghanaian congregations in the Netherlands and Germany, or the Nigerian congregations in Britain and in France. Whatever we do, when we talk about Western Christianity in the twenty-first century, we need to bear in mind that it is not all white and it does not only speak a European language. The body of Christians in the West today includes world Christians of all kinds, speaking Yoruba, Akan, Swahili, Mandarin, Filipino and many other languages.

More often than not, Christians from different parts of the world – Christians of different races and cultures – fail to get along. Divided churches become the natural outcome, based on varying combinations of reasons: race, theology, class, and many more. This clash of Christianities is the unfortunate reality of our contemporary Western Christian landscape. We end up with Asian, African, Latin American congregations in our cities, and as if that is not enough we separate further into smaller congregations shaped along national identities. That is why we see Zimbabwean, Kenyan, Ghanaian, Korean and Filipino congregations scattered across our cities. Our cross-cultural tensions can take passive-aggressive forms. Sometimes we just ignore one another; British Christians often continue to behave as if foreign Christians are not here – they continue with church business as usual, as if the demographic of their neighbourhoods has not changed. If foreign Christians seek to rent space from British churches, it becomes easy to deny them (often just to remind the foreign Christians that they are foreigners). Even if they are allowed to use the space, the two congregations may hardly meet and are unlikely to get to know one another and worship together. The renting of space is usually a business transaction that rarely leads to relationships between the congregations as they intentionally avoid each other. An African congregation in the Midlands lost their rental licence in 2018 because, as the official statement said, they were too loud, especially on Friday nights when they had their vigils. When they pushed to find out the real reason for having their licence revoked, it became clear that the issue was the 'smelly' foods they cooked in the church's kitchen. Fair enough – though I wondered if the two congregations could actually have had a conversation to find some middle ground solution that could enrich both of them.

At other times the clash takes the form of outright rejection of those Christians who do not look, speak, think or pray like us, in the belief that all those who are Christians will be like us and behave like us. If they are not like us, they are not Christian enough; in which case they must make an effort to become like us. If they are not willing to become like us, they are not welcome because their presence among us will change us – or cause us to change – and this is scary to many congregations. I have heard it countless times: 'those migrant Christians will force us to change the way we have done things for decades, and we are neither interested nor willing to do that'. Of course, change is difficult. We often refuse to accept strangers because no one wants to deal with change. We send strangers away, directing them to other churches to disguise our rejection of them and make it look like we actually care. A few years ago, when I was involved in training pastors for an African denomination in Birmingham, I sent my students to several white British churches in the neighbourhood on an assignment, to have them engage with Christians outside their own denomination. They all came back with the same report: 'we were told that we were welcome, but we were also informed that while we are welcome to come back there is an African church in the next town that could cater better for our needs'. The leaders may have been well-meaning, believing that maybe these Africans had needs that could not be met in a white-majority British congregation. However, the message that there is a church for 'people like you' down the road is unjustifiable in the twenty-first century. Those interested in growing multicultural congregations need to start from somewhere – with even one or two racially or culturally different families. Redirecting them, even if you mean well, appears like rejection and makes it difficult for people of other colours and races to stay.

The homogeneous unit principle

The immediate theological answer and its justification – for the dominant cultures of the West – has been found in Donald McGavran's homogeneous unit principle (HUP, widely expounded in his book of 1955, *The Bridges of God*).[3] Charles Peter Wagner, one of McGavran's fervent disciples, describes a homogeneous unit or people group as 'a section of society in which all the members have some characteristics in common'.[4] Such characteristics include language, nationality, race, tribe, caste or culture. While in India where he served as a missionary, McGavran observed that people liked to become Christians without crossing racial, linguistic or class barriers. He cites biblical and historical examples to support his argument such as the conversion of the Berean Jews (Acts 17.10–14) and the Christianizing of the Anglo-Saxons in 600 CE through the influence of Augustine upon the Kentish king, Ethelbert. This, to him, was evidence that group conversion is as necessary as individual conversion and is often more advantageous. He understood the phrase *panta ta ethne* ('all the nations') in the Great Commission of Matthew 28.19 as a reference to families, clans, tribes, castes and ethnic groups – that is, the 'peoples' of humanity. He reasoned that mission's objective, therefore, is to 'reach' each cultural group. He explains further:

> Humanity is a vast mosaic of tens of thousands of pieces ... Each segment must be won to Christ on its own level. If it is invited to join a church composed of people living on a different level, it will reject Christ very largely because the Saviour is obscured by his congregation ... The growth of the church will not melt green, white, black, yellow, purple, and red pieces of the mosaic into one dark grey piece. No, the red will remain red, the white will remain white, and the purple will remain purple. But each of the thousands of ethnic unit societies of the redeemed will multiply.[5]

McGavran initially saw this principle as a strategic way past India's formidable caste barriers, but he later developed it as a generic concept applicable to many fields. The principle is important for evangelism, in his estimation, because unbelievers understand the gospel better when expounded by their own kind of people. He contends that this issue of cross-cultural evangelism if not handled properly can keep whole societies out of eternal life due to offence.

HUP has been proven to work in many international scenarios, especially when foreign missionaries allow local Christians to lead the work of evangelism. However, Stephen Rhodes wisely worries that Christian leaders will rationalize segregation along homogeneous lines, arguing that homogeneous ministry is the only way out of decline – that multi-lingual ministry is a wonderful concept but not practical.[6] Criticism of the homogeneous unit principle and therefore of both assimilation and pluralism, and hence significant to the argument of this book, comes from John Perkins, an African American pastor:

> Today Christians study the science of withdrawing from others and then use it to attract converts ... It sugarcoats racial segregation with a veneer of spirituality and in practice continues the legacy of segregation

that divides whites and blacks into separate churches, relationships and agendas.[7]

John Root sanctions that the principle is 'impermissible' in Christianity. He argues that the New Testament Church transcended all forms of human barriers so that there was no longer 'Greek and Jew, circumcised and uncircumcised, barbarian, Scythian, slave and free; but Christ is all and in all' (Col. 3.11). He recaps Paul's admonition to Peter when he refused to eat with Gentiles in Galatians 2.11–16, indicating that this was meant to douse any ideas of ethnic or religious superiority among the brethren. He highlights that:

> The New Testament Christians were not prepared to separate ethnically in the hope of pushing on faster in preaching the Gospel; rather they saw that failure to achieve a practically expressed integration of believers, quite simply destroyed the Gospel they were commissioned to preach.[8]

He further points to the eschatological worship described in Revelation 7.9, where 'a great multitude that no one could count, from every nation, from all tribes and peoples and languages' stood before the throne as proof that God desires unity and diversity in worship. Commenting on the British situation, Root asserts that the widespread presence of 'black churches' is not merely a 'cultural' phenomenon as many white clergy prefer to believe. They are, in Root's opinion, a 'response to the experience of racism and oppression in British society'. He believes that negative and often media-induced stereotypes indicating that the mixing of different races is a recipe for violent conflict can be contradicted by a unified and racially mixed fellowship of Christians. In addition, 'white superiority or condescension will be muted by appreciating the contribution of Black Christians'.[9] He concludes that targeting or focusing on people's ethnic identity rather than their common humanity is hypocritical and causes awkwardness and self-consciousness. Many scholars reflecting on HUP in the twenty-first century agree that homogeneous groups are more exclusive than inclusive.

Describing British evangelicalism as largely middle class, Root blames this concept for the lack of growth in British Christianity. Indeed, it appears to me that HUP only Christianizes racism and endorses segregation, often serving to preserve the existence of ethnic groupings – a reality that is abominable to Christian conscience and unity. A good illustration of this is how homogeneous units failed to directly address the social injustice of the caste system in India. By targeting different castes for the benefit of the spread of the gospel, it maintained them. Of course, what HUP means for us today is that Africans will have their own churches, as do Ethiopians and Koreans. What may be worse, Swedish Lutherans will have their own church, not wanting to mix with German Lutherans. It is not surprising that there is little cross-breeding between these churches, even more so between these and the mainstream white churches.

The Pasadena Consultation (1978) of experts on this controversial subject (which included McGavran) aptly captured the predicament of the HUP thesis:

> In our commitment to evangelism, we all understand the reasons why homogeneous unit churches usually grow faster than heterogeneous or multicultural ones. Some of us, however, do not agree that the rapidity with which churches grow is the only or even always the most import-ant Christian priority. We know that an alien culture is a barrier to faith. But we also know that segregation and strife in the church are barriers to faith. If, then, we have to choose between apparent acqui-escence in segregation for the sake of numerical church growth and the struggle for reconciliation at the expense of numerical church growth, we find ourselves in a painful dilemma.[10]

Wayne McLintock made a sociological critique of McGavran's methods.[11] He postulated that McGavran's examples and conclusion that New Testament churches were largely mono-ethnic in nature is erroneous because his assumptions were purely based on biblical enquiry, thus neglecting other important sources of information. He adds that special-ists in the sociology of the New Testament period agree that believers in the churches founded by Paul were from all levels of society, and nowhere in the New Testament is there any substantial evidence to sup-port McGavran's claims. He suggests that McGavran used a selective reading of the Bible to validate his theoretical position.

Adding to the criticisms of HUP, Dan Sheffield in his book *The Multi-cultural Leader* talks about the cultural significance of class/status in shaping churches.[12] He observes that there are many monocultural multi-ethnic churches and he suggests that these may be the best way forward. In such churches, many people from different cultural back-grounds attend one church and they all live as part of one culture. In some cases, this is a transitional stage in the life of a congregation, for instance when a church that has been monocultural for much of its history then finds itself in a community undergoing social/cultural transformation. It still maintains its traditional cultural values, its familiar ways of worship and centralized power-sharing. However, this monocultural multi-ethnic church could simply be another way of doing 'assimilation'. In my opin-ion, the homogeneous unit principle is a sociological argument that lacks theological grounding. It works well under assimilation and pluralism, keeping people within their own cultural circles. An upgraded version of the homogeneous unit principle deals not only with the ethnically diverse communities but also with sub-groupings within the dominant culture, like 'Boomers' and 'GenXers', treating them as mono-cultural groups. That world has changed. While we are not dismissing the homogeneous strategies, we need to realize that they need to be accompanied by inten-tionally multicultural strategies as well.

How about a heterogeneous unit principle?

We are living in a multicultural world. While some places are more multi-cultural than others, there is more cultural and racial variety in the UK today than there was a generation ago, and cultural diversity is likely to continue to increase. However, it is still painfully true that 11 a.m. on Sunday morning is the most segregated hour of the week. Christian communities lag behind wider society on issues of diversity. While we may celebrate the rise of world Christianity, we also expect that these world Christians will congregate in their own groups based on cultural or national identity. It becomes acceptable for African churches and British churches to use the same premises but not see the need to be together. It appears abnormal when British and African Christians decide to worship together in one congregation. We have good excuses for this – 'that church is too quiet', or 'that church is too loud', or 'they sing the wrong type of songs', or 'they use the wrong version'. Many churches' response to cultural diversity has been shaped mostly by assimilation (at a congregational level) and cultural pluralism (for denominations). Both assimilation and pluralism make it difficult for the different Christian cultures to mix. Since minorities and immigrants are naturally expected to adopt the Western-shaped Christian culture and church, assimilation requires a letting go of beliefs and practices – or theologies – that the dominant culture finds strange, and cultural pluralism means that gather-ings of migrants are of secondary status as minority fellowships. Often, there is no link between these minority fellowships and the life of the con-gregation, exposing the patronizing sentiments that sometimes get such fellowships started.

Instead of following McGavran's homogeneous unit principle, it appears to me that in this age of cultural diversity we need to do the exact opposite, especially in contexts where people of different cultures (or races, classes, nationalities) live together. Congregations located in contexts of cultural diversity in the society must always seek to be multi-cultural if they are to reflect their contexts. They must be intentionally heterogeneous units, always attempting to reflect diversity in every aspect of their congregational life. Essentially, Christians in contexts of cultural diversity do not only need to figure out how best to share the gospel across cultures. We know that this is best done by people within the culture groups we are trying to reach. More important, they must also work out how to live and worship together as a community of people of many cultures, races and tribes. The questions that face us when we try to do this are a mirror that the gospel holds for us to see ourselves in God's light. Such questions always have to do with power: racial, tribal, cultural, economic, status. For instance, whose culture will be accepted as normative? What kind of songs will be used? What genres? What kind of food will be served at congregational gatherings? When we get to the bottom of all this, we find that we have to answer the question: 'Is fellowship with these people worth all the sacrifices that we will need to make?' If we do this well, we realize that a multicultural worshipping community is always a testament to the saving grace of Christ – the grace that enables us to belong together across many cultures in a world where racism, classism and many other dividing 'isms' reign.

A mission-shaped church is always influenced by the context in which it exists. When such a church is located in a context of cultural diversity, it must reflect the diversity in its membership, but it must also reflect diversity in its leadership. People belong where they identify, and they will identify when they feel truly represented in the circles of leadership and power. When this is done right, the congregation behaves in ways that actually make it possible for *others* to belong. This is critical. Multi-cultural congregations model for the world how racial reconciliation happens. The world needs to see that British people can belong together with Arabs, Asians, Africans and Latin Americans. Multicultural congregations can become a preview of what heaven may look like.

In addition, the best way to effectively engage a multicultural context in mission is through a multicultural missionary community. Otherwise, Christianity becomes a dividing force that socializes people into segregated congregations even though they live multiculturally at work, at school and practically everywhere else. Mission in Britain must, of necessity, involve all members of the body of Christ in Britain – and this must be done in unity. In other words, mission must involve the millions of migrant Christians living in Britain today. This is for several reasons. First, as the British populace is very culturally diverse, it needs the testimony of all peoples to fully see the gospel at work in their communities.

What a powerful testimony it is to know that the God that is at work among British people is also at work among Iranians in Manchester or Pakistanis in Birmingham or Zimbabweans in Sheffield, and among Malawians in Leicester, Nigerians in London and Brazilians in Oxford. Second, as argued earlier, migrant Christians bring with them gifts – like the penknife from Malawi – that may help unlock some areas of Britain for mission. Africans, for instance, bring their night vigils of fervent prayers and intercession and a zeal for evangelism. What a joy it would be if that zeal for evangelism were shared among all Christians in Britain. The re-evangelization of Britain will only be possible if all the gifts of the global Christians resident here are both received and released in mission. Could it be possible that a *heterogeneous* unit could help reshape our ecclesiology in ways that reflect the world we live in?

Notes

1 Robert D. Putnam, *Bowling Alone: The Collapse and Revival of American Community* (New York: Simon & Schuster, 2000).

2 Robert Neelly Bellah, *Habits of the Heart: Individualism and Commitment in American Life*, updated edn (Berkeley: University of California Press, 1996).

3 Donald Anderson McGavran, *The Bridges of God: A Study in the Strategy of Missions* (New York: Friendship Press, 1955).

4 C. Peter Wagner, *Strategies for Church Growth: Tools for Effective Mission and Evangelism* (Ventura, CA: Regal, 1987), p. 181.

5 Donald Anderson McGavran, *Effective Evangelism: A Theological Mandate* (Phillipsburg, NJ: Presbyterian and Reformed Pub. Co., 1988), pp. 111–13, 116.

6 Stephen A. Rhodes, *Where the Nations Meet: The Church in a Multicultural World* (Downers Grove, IL: InterVarsity Press, 1998), p. 76.

7 John Perkins, *Beyond Charity: The Call to Christian Community Development* (Grand Rapids, MI: Baker, 1993), p. 49.

8 John Root, 'Issues for the Church in a Multi-racial Society', *Themelios* 10, no. 2 (1985), p. 33.

9 Root, 'Issues for the Church in a Multi-racial Society', p. 34.

10 Lausanne Committee for World Evangelization, 'The Pasadena Consultation: Homogeneous Unit Principle (LOP 1)' (1978).

11 Wayne McLintock, 'Sociological Critique of the Homogeneous Unit Principle', *International Review of Mission* 77, no. 305 (1988), p. 107.

12 Dan Sheffield, *The Multicultural Leader: Developing a Catholic Personality* (Toronto: Clements, 2005).

10

Making Multiculturalism Work

Many realms of our lives as residents of these great British Isles are racially integrated. In most urban areas, it is impossible to find segregated spheres. Even though we tend to live in ethnically shaped communities, we have laws against racial discrimination in our housing. We have regulations that outlaw discrimination based on skin colour. Schools in neighbourhoods that are culturally diverse will reflect this diversity. In the marketplace and the workforce, racial discrimination is not tolerated. In sport and entertainment racism is banned. However, it is somewhat accepted as the norm for churches to be segregated even in multi-ethnic communities. As it is in America, it is also true in Britain that Sunday morning is still the most segregated hour as an overwhelming majority of congregations in multicultural communities are still monocultural in their membership. There is no real incentive for Christians and their congregations to work together across cultural and racial barriers. Those who attempt it, usually with the intention of being involved in God's mission – either to build a house of prayer for all nations or to recognize that even the host is also a stranger – find that it comes at a huge cost. It is certainly less complicated to focus on one culture or race as we establish congregations. The church growth movement has argued that monocultural churches grow faster. This request for us to find new ways to belong together in our ecclesiologies is countercultural in our contemporary world but, as argued earlier, multicultural worship is where we are coming from and where we are going.

The image of the future that John paints for us in Revelation 7 invites us to a future that God has ordained for us. We will worship together in eternity. There is nothing we can do about it. We will not be able to bring our racist tendencies to God's throne. The opportunities we have to engage one another in our multicultural neighbourhoods allow us to experience a foretaste of the future. However, John's image is not only about the future. In the kingdom of God, the future has broken into the present through the work of the Holy Spirit. While we celebrate the image as our eschatological future, we can live today as we will do then. We see and hear God better when the gifts of our colours come together to make a beautiful picture, as with a mosaic. Our worship will be a polyphony of glorious voices from every nation, tribe and tongue in unison even in our day and age. Nowhere else in the world is this more possible than in Britain.

The Christian population in Britain reflects the diversity that shapes the multicoloured body of Christ worldwide. The cultural diversity within the Christian community in Britain can never be overemphasized; it is possible to find Christians from every major people group in our cities. What shall we do with this diversity of races, worldviews, theologies and cultures? Unfortunately, cultural diversity is often ignored, sometimes wasted – our congregations are shaped in ways that amplify the voices of one culture, be it African (or Nigerian, Ghanaian, Kenya), British, Polish, Korean. When we look around at what is happening in congregations in our cities, it looks like multicultural churches are the anomaly. It seems that churches are unable to identify with more than one culture at a time.

The challenging thing about intercultural mutuality in the body of Christ is usually not the theological or liturgical differences. While they play a role in the shaping of Christian communities, they are generally easier to negotiate. People know what to do with strange theology or false doctrines. What we find difficult to deal with – and what we rarely talk about – are the sociocultural issues that shape our communities and have an impact on the way we congregate. One of these issues is that we still live with residual colonialism, and the doctrine of white/Western supremacy that provided the justification for slavery and the West's domination of the world continues to justify racism in some areas. Less than 40 years ago, Zimbabwe was still a British colony, and it was only 70 years ago that India gained independence from Britain. While many Christians reading this book may not think that the colour of their skin makes them superior or inferior to others, the truth (at least from the perspective of many African and Latin American pastors in Britain) is that race matters.

Race matters even though very few people actively choose to be racist. Even among Christians, however, racism is real. Usually it is covert but occasionally it shows its ugly head. Revival has come to Britain, but it looks like the messy migration of African and Caribbean Christians to Britain, and thus it does not look like revival at all. Most African pastors in Europe and North America mention race as the most difficult issue facing their ministries, and yet most of my white British middle-aged middle-class Christian friends say that racism is a thing of the past. Nevertheless, I am convinced that race will be a central issue in mission this century as the numbers of non-Western missionaries continue to rise and Christianity becomes increasingly darker in complexion. How then shall we make intercultural mutuality work? I propose that paying attention to the need to learn from, and about, each other and pursuing authentic cross-cultural relationships will be critical.

Oasis International

Oasis International[1] (OI) is a non-affiliated congregation of about 150 members in the Midlands. It is a part of a loosely connected fellowship of churches. Even though OI is non-affiliated denominationally, it is deeply Charismatic in its theology and outlook. It can easily pass for a Pentecostal congregation. It was started in 1930, and has seen many cycles of growth and decline since then. Its Charismatic roots go far back to the Charismatic revivals of the early 1900s, especially the Welsh Revivals of 1904. A major part of OI's identity stems from its feeling that God has called it to be a 'house of prayer for all nations'. Prior to adopting this as its theological framework for mission, it identified itself as 'a place where strangers become friends' and 'a place where everyone is somebody and Jesus is Lord'. Under the leadership of the current pastor, OI has started to see continued seasons of growth. It is situated in a residential area with a stable population. While the congregation has moved premises more than once in the last 90 years, it has always been situated within a one-mile radius of its original location. Current records show that OI has an African attendance of 31 per cent, a significant growth from 6 per cent reported 25 years ago. This has been a huge step in the direction of becoming a real house of prayer for the nations. Many of the non-white British members are immigrants, hailing from over 20 nations around the world.

A house of prayer for the nations

The fact that OI identifies itself as a 'house of prayer for all nations' provides the lens through which it looks at the world. Living out this idea has given them the ideological tools to help them be open to cultural diversity. They call themselves a 'small-ish' church but they have such a big heart and expansive vision. Their African and Asian members are active. They all feel they are at a good place where they can grow both in leadership and in the work of the ministry. When I visited them, one of their leaders told me, 'Here, you decide how much you want to get involved in anything, including leadership.' Another African leader added, 'No matter what your nationality or whatever, I think if you want to be a pastor; you end up as a pastor, if you want to just sit back, you can just sit back.'

In addition, there seemed to be a healthy mix of expressions of spiritualities in the church. Some Asian and African members told me (several times, actually) that when they walked into OI for the first time, it felt just like home. OI seems to have overcome the racial barriers that separate immigrants from British Christians. They are people of multicultural prayer, living out their vision to become a house of prayer for all nations. Prayer is very important to them; it envelops everything they do. Every prayer meeting is intentionally led by two or three people of different nationalities.

This 'fellowship of the Spirit' does not only occur within the premises of the church. Their hospitality takes place in their homes too. From the children's church to the international choir and the pulpit, it was clear that migrant Christians had taken some serious ownership of the church. Having journeyed with OI for three years, I can identify some of the key characteristics that make its multiculturalism work. Here are some of them.

Hospitality

First is the concept of multiculturalism and its relationship to hospitality within congregations. Indeed, even though hospitality was not something I expected to see, especially in a congregation that has 50 per cent white British and 50 per cent immigrants, I noticed very quickly how it was a very significant factor in multicultural Christian coexistence within congregations. This is more so because African immigrants and Westerners have different definitions of hospitality and therefore different expectations. What a Westerner may call a hospitable atmosphere may leave an African feeling entirely disconnected, and what an African may call hospitality may feel like a hostage situation to a Westerner. For instance, in many African cultures, a guest does not 'open their mouth' (among the aChewa of Malawi, *satsegula pakamwa*, and it is used figuratively to say the guest does not offer advice) until they are fully convinced of the invitation to do so. Westerners do not have such a rule. And because of something as simple as this, miscommunications happen quite regularly. Thus, hospitality is usually in the form of an invitation to engage in whatever conversations are taking place among the hosts. That is how one knows that these people have accepted the guests among themselves. Hospitality means speaking rights. Many Westerners do not have to feel 'at home' before they contribute in conversations. More important, they do not understand why Africans take so long before they feel at home enough to engage in deep conversations.

[handwritten margin note: meaning of an action looks different]

Among Malawians, the concept of *umunthu* is taught to children right from their early years. It is often demonstrated practically by teaching the toddlers to share not just their food but, more importantly, their toys. By the time they start school, most children will have learned that to have *umunthu* – or to be a *munthu* to be a person – is to be able to share with others, even those things one holds dear. Of course, in an ideal world all toys would be shared. However, that would take away one's power to share, which is where the power of *umunthu* lies.

In reflecting on cultural diversity and hospitality as seen in OI, the concept of *umunthu* becomes a useful hermeneutical tool. *Umunthu* encompasses the communal, moral and spiritual aspects of being human. To have *umunthu* is to be a communal and hospitable person. It speaks directly into the subject of cultural diversity and hospitality. This hospitality, for Malawians, is more than giving someone a bowl of soup and a place to sleep. It means to humanize the stranger by including them in the daily happenings in a community, treating them in the same way as one would someone who belongs to the community. To exclude is to dehumanize, and to dehumanize is to lack *umunthu*. As such, *umunthu* speaks rather directly about the status of the host and the stranger. The *umunthu* of the host is fulfilled in the humanizing of the stranger – and this humanizing is embodied in the act of treating the stranger the way they would treat their own. It is fulfilled in treating the stranger in the way the host would want to be treated if the roles were reversed. In *umunthu*, Africans find the embodiment of the commandment to love one's neighbour as oneself, especially when the neighbour is a stranger (Rom. 13.8–10). Hospitality, then, brings the host down to the level of the stranger, and at the same time elevates the stranger to the level of the host.

Umunthu says, 'you are human just like I am, and therefore I must treat you the way I would want to be treated'. It opens up the potential for equality and partnership between the host and the stranger. It means that the host and the stranger can have authentic and respectful conversations, each listening intently to the other. This is what genuine cultural diversity would look like: both the host and the stranger opening up their worlds for the possibility of something new and positive that their acting together may bring forward. It means that the host is sometimes the stranger and the stranger is sometimes the host – entailing the humanizing act of listening to one another. There is no room for the host to patronize the stranger. This is lived out every day throughout Malawi. The stranger is encouraged, or maybe one would say required, to participate in the activities of the host community. To use the metaphor of play, it is natural to tell the stranger, 'You cannot sit down and watch while we are playing. You must come and join us.' This offer of hospitality is never turned down. Even if the stranger does not know the game being played, he or she will participate in one way or another. In that way, the stranger is humanized and incorporated into the community.

I found the situation at OI very interesting. The migrant Christians owned the church just as much as everybody else at the church – the Chinese, the Koreans, the Nigerians. There was a sense in all the conversations that the immigrants were expected and encouraged to contribute at all levels to the life of the congregation. The leadership team includes an African, a Chinese, a Brazilian and a white British. No form of ministry is beyond reach. They are all so enthusiastic about mission and ministry at OI that one would wonder if they could ever fit in within an immigrant church. The theological theme, 'to be a house of prayer for all nations', has given them the tools to be excited about the stranger to the point of trusting them with leadership positions.

Learning to listen

We have to stay committed to listening to and learning from (and about) one another. If we do this well, we will discover at the end of the day that we are all human, wanting the same thing – and that the prejudice and insecurities are usually unfounded. This will help us create space where class, race and justice can be discussed without shame, guilt or condemnation. The more we learn about one another, the better our chances of successfully partnering for mission. Both sides need to listen to one another deeply to learn from one another and not to find weaknesses in each other's arguments. There are countless lessons to be learned from each other. I anticipate that there will be a need to engage people with some cross-cultural fluency to serve as interpreters – perhaps people who have lived in both cultures, or the children of migrants who have grown up and been educated in Britain.

Unfortunately, a great deal of the resources currently available for church planters assume that homogeneity is necessary for success. To grow churches, we are told, we need to target a homogeneous group of people with similar cultural characteristics because people do not like to cross-cultural barriers to belong in a church. However, John Perkins reminds us that:

Homogeneity does not mirror the image of God. It cheapens the people who proclaim it, and mocks God's call for us to be agents of reconciliation. What makes it even more harmful is how it is justified: 'If we are segregated, more people will come to hear the gospel, which in turn, advances the kingdom of God.' This logic spits in the face of a holy God by playing to our human weaknesses and sin nature. At the same time that it increases the size of our churches' membership, it retards our spiritual growth.[2]

The Malawian proverbs do not only talk about the need to listen to each other. They are about hospitality. Most of the listening and learning will take place in the context of fellowship. Of course, humanity thrives on hospitality and generosity – on being a welcoming community to the stranger. The absence of hospitality and generosity brings about isolation, that of both the guest and the host, and therefore diminishes life. The cultural diversity we see in British Christianity is a gift from God. Like the guest who brings a sharp penknife, migrant Christians come bearing gifts that may invigorate British Christianity and help re-evangelize the nation. To reap its benefits, it may be helpful to be intentional in our response.

Cross-cultural relationships

Leaders on both sides of the conversation need to model cross-cultural partnerships for their followers. They need to show their people what it looks like to respectfully recognize and work with people that look different from them. Western leaders need to go out of their way to make their 'home ground' conducive to immigrants to engage with others. African leaders need to be willing to engage in true relationships with British Christians even when they disagree with them on some issues. This will need something more radical than the sharing of pulpits and inviting one another for events and conferences – though that is a good starting point. For it to succeed, they need organic and authentic friendships that go beyond church events. We need to focus on forming real cross-cultural relationships, and partnerships will follow. Many start with partnerships and wonder why very few relationships are formed along the way.

Central to the discussion of British and foreign Christians worshipping together is the issue of power: the power that the host has to choose between being hospitable or not, choosing between engaging the foreigner or not, and after the initial engagement the power to 'level the playing field' such that foreigners can share the power in leadership roles. The Spirit democratizes the gifts between the host and the stranger. However, it is usually difficult for the hosts to allow foreigners into leadership positions among them. As hosts, British Christians will often find that they have a bigger role to play. The power of being the host can be a barrier to cultural diversity; to be good hosts, we have to be open to being vulnerable with one another. The host needs to be able to depend on the migrant in one way or another. Our congregations will have to learn to be vulnerable, to depend on God and the stranger for their being. Luke 10 tells of the disciples having to depend on the hospitality of the stranger for their ministry. The bringer of the gift has to depend on the hospitality of the one who needs the gift.

Theology in a post-colonial and multicultural world

We will need to develop new theological tools that look at faith, race and mission in healthy ways that encourage cross-racial missional partnerships. We need a theology that will discredit the racial prejudices that prevail in the Church today. In Christ, race should not matter. The future of Christianity is multiracial and looks more like the robe that Jacob made for his son Joseph – a robe of many colours. Some denominations will have to embrace diversity because of the need to survive, largely using assimilation to keep the colours in the ranks, even if it means having a few token minorities in the leadership. Others will do it because of the missional call to be a prayer house for all nations. Whatever the case, European Christianity is becoming less European and more African, Asian and Latino by the year. Becoming a truly multicultural body of Christ in Britain does not mean having to resolve all cultural or theological differences, or iron out diversities. It is more about following God's Spirit into the future. The Church, in its variegated global manifestations, is an expression of the work of the Spirit of the Father who is the Spirit of Christ. This one Spirit is poured out upon *all* flesh, irrespective of ethnicity. God does not favour one ethnicity over another. The fact that the same Spirit is poured out on all Christians wherever they come from in the world has the most to teach us. The same Spirit can use whatever vessel is ready and available without consideration of colour or ethnicity. We should thus be ready to receive of the Spirit in spite of the colour of the vessel.

Authentically multicultural Christian communities will be open to hear, to dialogue with, to learn from and to encourage people of different cultures. This catholic personality realizes that while they may be of one particular culture the Holy Spirit has baptized them into the body of Christ, which is made up of people of many cultures, none of which is superior. A truly multicultural congregation will have room for many cultures to thrive within it, at the same time helping them to realize that together they make what the Church is.

When we read Ephesians 2, we generally look at it as a text about the reconciliation of two races: Jews and Gentiles. It often speaks powerfully to situations of racial division. However, when Paul wrote these words he was also talking about two cultures, within the context of the Church – about two contrasting lifestyles. These two cultures that had once been antagonistic to each other were put side by side at the institution that embodied the cultural and ethnic division that had prevailed before – at the fellowship meal table. The followers of Jesus in Ephesus and else-where in the New Testament world shared meals together. At first among Jewish followers of the Way in Palestine the meal served to include all as equal members of the *ekklesia* while at the same time reshaping the power structures, making Palestinian Jews and Hellenistic Jews equal participants in the kingdom of Christ. As time passed, Gentile Christians joined the fellowship, and the table of Communion included them too and made them rightful participants in the kingdom. The fact that Jews and Gentiles sat together at the table is no small matter. This 'breaking bread together' was foundational to their faith. Table fellowship was at the centre of their self-understanding, but centuries of Jewish history had said that Jews do not sit at table with Gentiles. Even Peter (Gal. 2.11–14), much later in his life and ministry, struggled with this. How could he, as a Jew, break bread with the Gentiles?

All in all, multicultural worshipping communities need to learn new habits and practices that enforce their commitment to cultural diversity. They cannot continue to live in a monocultural mode while expecting to be multicultural. Like Peter, they must learn that sometimes God tells us not to 'call unclean something God calls clean' and to eat with the Gentiles even when it goes against everything we believed to be right. This new humanity – or tribe – that God is creating out of us requires that we let go of some cultural habits in order to embrace new ones.

Notes

1 Oasis International ministries is a fictitious composite image of three multi-cultural churches that I have visited a few times over the past three years. I visited them because I was invited to speak about multicultural leadership. Having jour-neyed with them for this time, I have had the opportunity to observe them closely to see what makes their multiculturalism work. What I give here is a brief report of what I saw.

2 John Perkins, *Beyond Charity: The Call to Christian Community Develop-ment* (Grand Rapids, MI: Baker, 1993), p. 49.

11

Monocultural Churches in a Multicultural World

The term monocultural churches is generally used to describe monoracial churches, and multicultural churches tends to mean multiracial churches. The terms are used interchangeably. However, it is best to understand 'culture' here in a more holistic manner. Culture is a composite of many things, and while race may be one of them, race is not equal to culture. When we talk about monocultural and multicultural churches, we need to think beyond race. A middle-class suburban church can be mono-cultural even though it is racially mixed, while a church with a mixture of classes can be multicultural even though it is made up of one race.

Why do monocultural churches exist?

There are valid reasons for the existence of monocultural churches. To begin with, most first-generation migrants find that mastering a new language is difficult, especially if they are older. They may need space to worship in a language they can understand and this will generally be in a monocultural church. Another reason is that in some rural towns and villages around the country racial diversity is non-existent. Then there is a theory among church planting and church growth enthusiasts that suggests that churches grow faster if they are monocultural. Church planters are encouraged to find their niche – people of similar cultural characteristics to them – if their church plant is to grow fast, because people like to attend churches where they do not need to cross-cultural barriers. Unfortunately, this kind of thinking shapes a great deal of evangelical church planting today. In addition, some pastors believe that God has sent them a specific people group and nobody else. A Nigerian pastor in London assured me that he had no interest at all in reaching anybody who is not Nigerian simply because God had instructed him that his ministry was 'to preserve the Nigerians in Britain'. There are not many who think like this though.

The history of this ecclesial segregation in Britain goes back to the early days of the Windrush generation when migrants from the West Indies came to Britain in the years after World War Two. Being Christians who had come to the faith in a British colony and mostly through the work of British missionaries, they hoped that Britain, a Christian nation, would be hospitable and that they would be welcomed. That hope was dashed when they arrived, with deep anti-black sentiments being revealed in the populace. Many of that generation say that racism was also prevalent in the Church. Where they were made welcome, they found British Christianity relatively less enthusiastic and less expressive compared to churches in their homeland. In response, they formed their own churches. Many African Christians in Britain say that this racially charged rejection is still prevalent and shapes a great deal of their experiences when they try to join British churches.

They are here to stay

Monoracial churches will continue to exist as they are safe, convenient and comfortable. In a world that rewards those who make the most out of the path of least resistance, the difficult work of cross-cultural mission is not very attractive. I have heard pastors complain that the energy needed to lead a congregation of several cultural groups is unjustifiably enormous. There are too many pitfalls. What do you do when one cultural group has problems with another group's way of doing things? How do you make sure that all groups feel heard and have a place at the table? I remember one friend wondering, as an Englishman, whether to express the exuberance his Ghanaian members expect of their pastor when they have their naming ceremonies. A Zimbabwean pastor found that when white people came to his church, they complained that his preaching was too loud. Both local and foreign pastors find it too difficult to work across different races, and to avoid this they would rather stick with a situation where there is no need to cross cultural barriers.

However, monoracial churches create a bubble that allows people to get together in worship without having to attend to the needs of their neighbours who are different from them. If they do respond to their neighbourhoods, it is usually in the form of charity – offering help but not an invitation to church. Perhaps, the wealthy would prefer to keep their less well-off neighbours out. Black folk might actively want to keep the white people out ('we cannot let them dominate us in our worship too'), and white people want to keep black people out ('they bring issues that we don't have time for'). Ironically, British churches will send missionaries to Africa while neglecting their African neighbours on their streets in Britain.

Mission and the monocultural Church

Monocultural churches, especially in contexts of cultural diversity, go against everything we read in the New Testament. Christianity emerged in a multicultural context. Acts 2 is a multinational adventure that engages the entire Jewish diaspora of the day. The disciples spoke great things of God in tongues that were translated in the ears of the hearers into many languages from around the world. Later, in Acts 11, the word 'Christian' was coined to describe the multicultural fellowship of followers of the Way, as Jews and Gentiles joined together in worship. The arguments we hear justifying monocultural churches would never hold water among Antioch Christians whose leadership team was multicultural, or the saints in Ephesus who were advised by Paul that there is only one body and one Spirit (of Christ in the world) and the Galatian Christians who were reminded that 'you are all one in Christ' (Eph. 4.4; Gal. 3.28).

Monocultural churches in multicultural contexts paint an image of a God who pays attention to the needs of one racial or cultural group and not the others. They may argue that if God cares about the others, he will send other evangelists who look like them. More often than not, such monocultural churches will have a quasi-theological justification that supports their practice of a racist form of Christianity. 'This is how we reach the most people,' their church growth consultants say. However, in their practice of ecclesial segregation such churches preach of a God who is selectively movable, and church members tend not to be touched by the spiritual condition of those who are different from them. If the size of a congregation is what matters most to a minister, it is possible that he or she has substituted capitalism for God.

If we don't fix our eyes on the missionary God who gave his only Son to be crucified, and the missionary Son who became a slave for us to belong in the *ekklesia*, and the missionary Spirit who loves to be with the marginalized, we will justify racism, calling it good missionary practice. Migrants who say that worship feels better and more authentic in their mother tongue need to be reminded that mission only works in the language of the strangers that you are trying to evangelize. A commitment to stick to 'home languages' automatically excludes all who cannot speak the language – and this often includes their own sons and daughters. I know of several African denominations whose congregations here in Britain worship in Akan, Yoruba, Lingala or Kiswahili, and I often wonder how they can exclude and evangelize British people at the same time. Because of this, I am convinced that monocultural churches will have a short shelf-life, and last only for maybe a generation or two.

Racism, even Christian segregation, should have no place in growing the kingdom of God. It should not be a part of any church growth strategy. When the earth is transformed and creation redeemed, we will worship together – migrants and locals, black and white, rich and poor – across every dividing barrier. There will be no space for monocultural worship. The visions given to us in the book of Revelation show multitudes of people from every tribe and tongue worshipping together. That is where we are going. Maybe we can experiment with a foretaste of what that will be like. I am convinced that once a congregation goes multicultural, there is no going back.

Bibliography

Achebe, Chinua, *Things Fall Apart*, New York: McDowell, 1959.

Arbuckle, Gerald A., *Earthing the Gospel: An Inculturation Handbook for Pastoral Workers*, Maryknoll, NY: Orbis, 1990.

Baines, Dudley, *Emigration from Europe, 1815–1930*, New Studies in Economic and Social History, New York: Cambridge University Press, 1995.

Barrett, David B., Todd M. Johnson, Christopher R. Guidry and Peter F. Crossing, *World Christian Trends, AD 30–AD 2200: Interpreting the Annual Christian Megacensus*, Pasadena, CA: William Carey Library, 2001.

Bediako, Kwame, *Christianity in Africa: The Renewal of a Non-Western Religion*, Maryknoll, NY: Orbis, 1995.

Bellah, Robert Neelly, *Habits of the Heart: Individualism and Commitment in American Life*, updated edn, Berkeley, CA: University of California, 1996.

Berger, Peter L., *The Desecularization of the World: Resurgent Religion and World Politics*, Grand Rapids, MI: Eerdmans, 1999.

Beti, Mongo, *The Poor Christ of Bomba*, Long Grove, IL: Waveland, 1971.

Bosch, David J., *Transforming Mission: Paradigm Shifts in Theology of Mission*, American Society of Missiology Series, Maryknoll, NY: Orbis, 1991.

Brierley, Peter W., *London's Churches Are Growing! What the London Church Census Reveals*, Tonbridge: ADBC Publishers, 2013.

—— *Pulling out of the Nose Dive: A Contemporary Picture of Church Going: What the 2005 English Church Census Reveals*, Tonbridge: ADBC Publishers, 2006.

Carey, William, *An Enquiry into the Obligations of Christians to Use Means for the Conversion of the Heathens*, London: Carey Kingsgate, 1961.

Carter, Craig A., *Rethinking Christ and Culture: A Post-Christendom Perspective*, Grand Rapids, MI: Brazos Press, 2006.

Castles, Stephen and Mark J. Miller, *The Age of Migration: International Population Movements in the Modern World*, 4th edn, New York: Guilford Press, 2009.

Chaves, Mark, *Congregations in America*, Cambridge, MA: Harvard University Press, 2004.

Commission on World Mission and Evangelism and Ronald Kenneth Orchard, *Witness in Six Continents: Records of the Meeting of the Commission on World Mission and Evangelism of the World Council of Churches Held in Mexico City, December 8th to 19th, 1963*, London: Edinburgh House Press, 1964.

Conrad, Joseph, Fiona Banner and Paolo Pellegrin, *Heart of Darkness*, London: Four Corners, 2015.

DeYmaz, Mark, *Building a Healthy Multi-Ethnic Church: Mandate, Commitments, and Practices of a Diverse Congregation*, San Francisco, CA: Jossey-Bass, 2007.

Diamant, Jeff, and The Pew Research Centre, *The Countries with the 10 Largest Christian Populations and the 10 Largest Muslim Populations*, www.pewresearch.org/fact-tank/2019/04/01/the-countries-with-the-10-largest-christian-populations-and-the-10-largest-muslim-populations/.

Elizondo, Virgilio P., *The Future Is Mestizo: Life Where Cultures Meet*, Meyer-Stone (ed.), Oak Park, IL: Meyer-Stone, 1988.

Espinosa, Gastón, *Latino Pentecostals in America: Faith and Politics in Action*, Cambridge, MA: Harvard University Press, 2014.

Frost, Michael and Alan Hirsch, *The Shaping of Things to Come: Innovation and Mission for the 21st-Century Church*, Peabody, MA: Hendrickson, 2003.

Gatu, John, *Joyfully Christian and Truly African*, Nairobi: Acton, 2006.

Gerloff, Roswith, *A Plea for British Black Theologies: The Black Church Movement in Britain in Its Transatlantic Cultural and Theological Interaction with Special References to the Pentecostal Oneness (Apostolic) and Sabbatarian Movements*, Studien Zur Interkulturellen Geschichte Des Christentums, Frankfurt am Main: P. Lang, 1992.

Goheen, Michael W., *Introducing Christian Mission Today: Scripture, History, and Issues*, Downers Grove, IL: IVP Academic, 2014.

Hastings, Adrian, *A History of African Christianity, 1950–1975*, African Studies Series 26, Cambridge: Cambridge University Press, 1979.

Jenkins, Philip, *The Next Christendom: The Coming of Global Christianity*, 3rd edn, New York: Oxford University Press, 2011.

Jivraj, Stephen, *How Has Ethnic Diversity Grown 1991–2001–2011?*, Manchester: University of Manchester, 2012.

Johnson, Todd, Gina Zurlo, Albert Hickman and Peter Crossing, 'Christianity 2018: More African Christians and Counting Martyrs', *International Bulletin of Mission Research* 42, no. 1 (2018), pp. 20–8.

Kendall, R. Elliott, *The End of an Era: Africa and the Missionary*, London: SPCK, 1978.

Kim, Rebecca Y., *The Spirit Moves West: Korean Missionaries in America*, Oxford: Oxford University Press, 2015.

Kwiyani, Harvey C., 'Mission in the Global South', in *Missional Conversations: A Dialogue between Theory and Praxis in World Mission*, Cathy Ross and Colin Graham Smith (eds), London: SCM Press, 2018.

—— *Sent Forth: African Missionary Work in the West*, American Society of Missiology Series, Maryknoll, NY: Orbis, 2014.

Latourette, Kenneth Scott, *The Emergence of a World Christian Community*, New Haven, CT: Yale University Press, 1949.

Lausanne Committee for World Evangelization, 'The Pasadena Consultation: Homogeneous Unit Principle (Lop 1)', 1978.

McGavran, Donald Anderson, *The Bridges of God: A Study in the Strategy of Missions*, New York: Friendship Press, 1955.

McLintock, Wayne, 'Sociological Critique of the Homogeneous Unit Principle', *International Review of Mission* 77, no. 305 (1988), pp. 107–15.

Micklethwaite, John and Adrian Wooldridge, *God is Back: How the Global Revival of Faith is Changing the World*, New York: Penguin, 2009.

Mott, John R., *The Evangelization of the World in This Generation*, New York: Student Volunteer Movement for Foreign Missions, 1900.

New Life Covenant Church, 'Our Church: Our Leadership', 2019, www.mynew life.org/our-church-extended.

Oliphant, Anderson and Ferrier, *World Missionary Conference, 1910. Report of Commission One: Carrying the Gospel to All the Non-Christian World*, Edinburgh: 1910.

Olofinjana, Israel O., 'The Significance of Multicultural Churches in Britain: A Case Study of Crofton Park Baptist Church', in *Churches, Blackness, and Contested Multiculturalism: Europe, Africa, and North America*, R. Drew Smith, William Ackah and Anthony G. Reddie (eds), pp. 75–85, New York: Palgrave Macmillan, 2014.

Olusoga, David, *Black and British: A Forgotten History*, London: Macmillan, 2016.

Onishi, Norimitsu, 'Korean Missionaries Carrying Word to Hard-to-Sway Places', *The New York Times* (New York), 2004. www.nytimes.com/2004/11/01/world/asia/korean-missionaries-carrying-word-to-hardtosway-places.html?_r=0.

Pascale, Richard T., Mark Millemann and Linda Gioja, *Surfing the Edge of Chaos: The Laws of Nature and the New Laws of Business*, New York: Crown Business, 2000.

Perkins, John, *Beyond Charity: The Call to Christian Community Development*, Grand Rapids, MI: Baker, 1993.

Philips, Tom, 'China on Course to Become "World's Most Christian Nation" within 15 Years', *The Telegraph* (London), 2014.

Putnam, Robert D., *Bowling Alone: The Collapse and Revival of American Community*, New York: Simon & Schuster, 2000.

Rhodes, Stephen A., *Where the Nations Meet: The Church in a Multicultural World*, Downers Grove, IL: InterVarsity Press, 1998.

Ross, Kenneth R., '"Blessed Reflex" : Mission as God's Spiral of Renewal', *International Bulletin of Missionary Research* 27, no. 4 (2003), pp. 162–8.

Sheffield, Dan, *The Multicultural Leader: Developing a Catholic Personality*, Toronto: Clements, 2005.

Sherwood, Marika, *Pastor Daniels Ekarte and the African Churches Mission, Liverpool, 1931–1964*, London: Savannah Press, 1994.

Shorter, Aylward, *Toward a Theology of Inculturation*, Maryknoll, NY: Orbis, 1989.

Stanley, Brian, *The World Missionary Conference, Edinburgh 1910*, Studies in the History of Christian Missions, Grand Rapids, MI: Eerdmans, 2009.

Stanley, Henry M., *Through the Dark Continent: Or, the Sources of the Nile around the Great Lakes of Equatorial Africa, and Down the Livingstone River to the Atlantic Ocean*, 2 vols, New York: Harper, 1878.

Strohbehn, Ulf, *Pentecostalism in Malawi: A History of the Apostolic Faith Mission in Malawi, 1931–1994*, Kachere Theses, Zomba, Malawi: Kachere Series, 2005.

Sturge, Mark, *Look What the Lord Has Done!: An Exploration of Black Christian Faith in Britain*, Bletchley: Scripture Union, 2005.

Sundkler, Bengt and Christopher Steed, *A History of the Church in Africa*, Studia Missionalia Upsaliensia 74, New York: Cambridge University Press, 2000.

Taylor, Charles, *A Secular Age*, Cambridge, MA: Belknap Press of Harvard University Press, 2007.

Taylor, Charles and Amy Gutmann, *Multiculturalism: Examining the Politics of Recognition*, Princeton, NJ: Princeton University Press, 1994.

Temple, William, *The Church Looks Forward*, New York: Macmillan, 1944.

The PEW Forum on Religion and Public Life, *Global Christianity: A Report on the Size and Distribution of the World's Christian Population*, Washington DC: Pew Research Center, 2011.

Uka, Emele Mba, *Missionaries Go Home?: A Sociological Interpretation of an African Response to Christian Missions*, New York: Lang, 1989.

Volf, Miroslav, *Exclusion and Embrace: A Theological Exploration of Identity, Otherness, and Reconciliation*, Nashville, TN: Abingdon Press, 1996.

Wagner, C. Peter, *Strategies for Church Growth: Tools for Effective Mission and Evangelism*, Ventura, CA: Regal Books, 1987.

Walls, Andrew F., 'Of Ivory Towers and Ashrams: Some Reflections on Theological Scholarship in Africa', *Journal of African Christian Thought* 3, no. 1 (2000).

Welker, Michael, *God the Spirit*, Minneapolis, MN: Fortress Press, 1994.

Wood, Phil and Charles Landry, *The Intercultural City: Planning for Diversity Advantage*, London: Earthscan, 2008.

Zizioulas, John, *Being as Communion: Studies in Personhood and the Church*, Contemporary Greek Theologians, Crestwood, NY: St Vladimir's Seminary Press, 1985.

Index

Putnam, Robert 122

Racism 9, 68, 130, 133, 135–136, 145–146
Rebmann, Johannes 2
Redeemed Christian Church of God (RCCG) 12, 13, 43, 52, 53, 58, 126
  mission statement 53
  the Festival of Life of the RCCG 29
  the Holy Ghost Convention of the RCCG 29
  its Yoruba heritage 112, 124
Revival 49, 51, 54, 58–59, 136–137
Rhodes, Stephen 129
Root, John 130

Sanneh, Lamin 125
Secular humanism 34
Secularism 9, 18, 34, 60
Septuagint 80
Sheffield, Dan 131
Stanley, Brian 21
Summer Road Chapel 17

Tambaram 28
Taylor, Charles 60, 73
Temple, William 15, 17
Trans-Atlantic slave trade 19, 43, 46, 64
Tribalism
  the folly of 121, 123–124
Trinitarian theology 78, 95

Ubuntu 121
Umunthu 121, 139

Unity in diversity 78, 91, 98

Volf, Miroslav 96–97

Wagner, Charles P. 128
Walls, Andrew 29, 125
Welcome 5, 52, 69, 77, 87–88, 106, 114, 116, 128
Welker, Michael 96
Willingen 24, 28
Windrush
  migration from the West Indies 17
  SS Empire Windrush 44
  hostile environment 49
  generation 44, 74, 145
Wooldridge, Adrian 37
World Missionary Conference 6, 21
  African delegates at 21, 25
  Africa expected to convert to Islam 25
  Boston 26
  Cape Town 25
  Edinburgh 1910 21
  Edinburgh 2010 25
  Tokyo 26
World Christianity 15, 19–21
  its emergence 15–17

Xenolalia 103, 104

Yang, Fenggang 30

Zeus 84
Zizioulas, John 95
Zurlo, Gina 32

CPSIA information can be obtained
at www.ICGtesting.com
Printed in the USA
BVHW030802160821
614497BV00004B/65

9 780334 057529